THE GUILD STATE

To the craftsmen, both professional and amateur, who will provide the foundation of the Christian Guild State of the future.

$\mathcal{T}$he $\mathcal{G}$UILD STATE

ITS PRINCIPLES AND POSSIBILITIES

by

G. R. Stirling Taylor

Norfolk, VA
2006

The Guild State.
Copyright © 2006 IHS Press.
First published in 1919 by George Allen & Unwin, Ltd., of London.
Preface, footnotes, typesetting, layout, and cover design copyright
2006 IHS Press. All rights reserved.
The Guild State was originally published in 1919 by George Allen
& Unwin, Ltd., of London. The spelling, punctuation, and format-
ting of the original edition have been largely preserved. The text has
been slightly abridged and corrected editorially. Images of guild seals
and other illustrations are taken from *The Guilds of Dublin* by John J.
Webb, M.A., Ll.D. (New York/London: Kennikat Press, 1970, originally 1929). The image of Stirling Taylor on the back cover is taken
from the stained-glass "Fabian Window," designed by G.B. Shaw
and executed by Caroline Townshend in 1910, and now located in the
Shaw Library at the London School of Economics.

ISBN 1-932528-00-8

Library of Congress Cataloging-in-Publication Data

Taylor, George Robert Stirling.
    The guild state : its principles and possibilities / by G. R. Stirling
Taylor.
        p. cm.
Originally published: London : G. Allen & Unwin, 1919.
    ISBN 1-932528-00-8
    1. Guild socialism. I. Title.
    HD6479.T3 2004
    335'.15--dc21

                                                    2003013270

Printed in the United States of America.

IHS Press is the only publisher dedicated exclusively to the social
teachings of the Catholic Church. For more information, contact:
IHS Press
222 W. 21st St., Suite F-122
Norfolk, VA 23517
info@ihspress.com
www.ihspress.com
877-IHS-PRESS

Table of Contents

ST. AUDOEN'S ARCH

✻

ONE OF THE OLD GATES OF DUBLIN
WHERE MANY GUILDS HAD THEIR
MEETING PLACE

PUBLISHER'S PREFACE

"I am glad, therefore, that I said and wrote what is before the public, even though for a time some men have called me a Socialist and a revolutionist, and have fastened upon a subordinate consequence, and neglected the substance of my contention in behalf of the natural rights of the poor."

—Henry Edward Cardinal Manning, 1888

 T IS NOT SURPRISING that "true believers" in the free-market heresy reject the notion that *all* economic life is bound by ethics, and should be limited by the regulations of a guild system like that of the Middle Ages. They defend a social order antithetical to that advocated both by the greatest Catholic minds of the past and, in general terms, by the Church herself. But Catholics who take this same line—whether well-intentioned but uninformed, or partisans of that *laissez-faire* liberalism condemned by the modern Popes—are objectively an embarrassment to the Catholic cause.

The embarrassment stems as much from their deceit about what it is they oppose as from their disloyalty to the doctrine of the Popes who, for over a century, have urged a return to the principles behind the social institutions of the Age of Faith.* "Socialism!" is the first cry of many who reject the Distributist ideal of widespread ownership and its defense by a guild system nurturing small crafts and enforcing quality production, healthy and rewarding work, and—its centerpiece—the just price. Adding fuel to the

---

* Pope St. Pius X, in his famous reference to "traditionalists" as the "true friends of the people," was referring not to Latin-Mass Catholics, but rather to those advocating restoration of the guild system. As he notes just prior to the well-known passage: " . . . all that is needed is to take up again, with the help of the true workers for a social restoration, the organisms which the Revolution shattered, and to adapt them, in the same Christian spirit that inspired them, to the new environment arising from the material development of today's society" (*Notre Charge Apostolique*, August 15, 1910).

fire of calumny is the fact that some of the guildsmen and Distributists in the early 1900's used the term "socialism" to express (however vaguely) their opposition to the social Darwinism of the period, and still today historians – blind to their *sui generis* Catholic ethos – call A. J. Penty and G. R. Stirling Taylor "guild socialists."

The antidote to all this is *the truth*. The historical reality, the teaching of the Church, and the background of the socialists-turned-guildsmen prove that there was an abyss separating collectivists (the *real* Marxian socialists) advocating state ownership of productive property from guildsmen demanding, as Taylor does in *The Guild State*, social organization by function, decentralization, personal control and ownership of small industry, and the subordination of economic life to the needs of men. Both of these camps sometimes used the term "socialism"; but only a malcontent or a sophist would argue a necessary similarity of aim from a similarity of semantics, especially when the aims are as different as night and day.

Independent witness from unimpeachable Catholics proves that the "socialism" that men like Chesterton, Penty, Taylor, Maurice Reckitt, Fr. Vincent McNabb, and others were associated with (by themselves or others) had no relation at all to the materialist collectivism condemned by the Church. Fr. Edward Kiernan's dissertation for the Catholic University of America noted that "anyone who was not in agreement with the prevailing social and economic philosophy was liable to term himself or be called a Socialist . . . ."* Fr. Peter Coffey, onetime Professor at Maynooth in Ireland, and one of the country's "most eminent Catholic intellectuals,"† wrote,

> The word "socialist" is so elastic in its meaning that the day is past when any man or any man's teaching can be condemned . . . merely because [he or it] has been described as "socialist" by himself or by others. Whatever the adjective applied . . . [an economic system] has got to be examined on its merits before any ethical judgement can fairly be pronounced upon it.‡

---

* "Arthur J. Penty: His Life and Early Influences," *The Gauntlet* (Norfolk: IHS Press, 2003), p. 16, originally published on pp. 1–12 of *Arthur J. Penty: His Contribution to Social Thought* (Washington, D.C.: Catholic University of America, 1941).

† Dr. Brian Murphy, O.S.B., *The Catholic Bulletin and Republican Ireland* (Belfast: Athol Books, 2005), p. 182. Coffey's doctorate was from the Louvain in Belgium, 1905.

‡ "James Connolly's Campaign Against Capitalism," *The Catholic Bulletin*, April-

Fr. Bede Jarrett said much the same: "[m]any who ten years ago would have objected to [socialism] as a name of ill-omen see in it now nothing which may not be harmonized with the most ordinary of political and social doctrines."* And in *The Social Catholic Movement in Great Britain*, Georgiana McEntee writes that "[s]ocialism is a hydra-headed ideal, meaning widely different things to different people . . . . "† Quoting an exchange of letters in the New York *Evening Mail* between Frs. McNabb and John A. Ryan, she notes the priests' agreement that Leo XIII condemned "orthodox regular socialism" but left untouched other forms of the theory such as "Guild Socialism, Christian Socialism, Revisionist Socialism . . . . "‡

Though Pius XI thereafter declared that "no one can be at the same time a good Catholic and a true socialist" (*Quadragesimo Anno* (*QA*), 1931, §120), the question remains: what is a "true" socialist, and which doctrines are therefore condemned by the Church's teaching, and which proposed and defended by it?

In *QA* Pius XI *defines* socialism, condemning its "concept of society" as "utterly foreign to Christian truth" (§117). According to that truth, "man . . . is placed on this earth so that . . . by faithfully fulfilling the duties of his craft or other calling he may obtain for himself temporal and at the same time eternal happiness." Alternatively, "Socialism . . . [is] indifferent to this sublime end of both man and society, [and] affirms that human association has been instituted for the sake of material advantage alone" (§118).

With this definition, Pius XI made "Christian socialism" a "contradictory term" (§120) and eliminated the ambiguity that Catholic writers had lamented.§ Yet we can profit from studying

---

August, 1920, pp. 223–4, quoted in Murphy, p. 183.

* *Medieval Socialism* (London: Burns, Oates, and Washbourne, Ltd., 1935, reprinted from the 1913 edition), pp. 6–7.

† New York: The Macmillan Co., 1927, pp. 94–5.

‡ McEntee, p. 110.

§ C. S. Devas wrote: "[S]ocialism is often used in a loose sense to express any effort to prevent or to mitigate the evils of industrial life . . . . But this use of the term deprives it of all scientific value" (*The Key to the World's Progress* (London et al: Longmans, Green, & Co., 1924), p. 43). Victor Cathrein, S.J., pointed out that "in French and English, 'socialism' is also often spoken of as 'collectivism'" (*Socialism* (New York: Benzinger Bros., 1904), p. 21). According to Romano Amerio, the *idea* of a Christian socialism is in fact legitimate (*Iota Unum* (Kansas City: Sarto House, 1996), p. 265).

how the Distributists and their allies dealt with the issue, when many "socialist" circles included not just enemies of Christianity but men who were – however ignorant of the Social Teaching – striving for economic justice.* Honorable and constructive discussion was possible, *even though men disagreed*: Distributists refined their understanding, and "socialists" were exposed to Catholic social principles (through which Hamish Fraser and Douglas Hyde came into the Church a generation later). This kind of engagement by Catholics followed the teaching of St. Paul to "prove all things; hold fast that which is good" (1 Thess. v:21) and Pius XI (to those wishing to be "apostles among socialists") to strive "to show . . . that socialist claims, so far as they are just, are far more strongly supported by the principles of Christian faith . . . " (*QA*, §116).

To that end, Distributists and guildsmen like Hilary Pepler, Belloc, Cecil and G. K. Chesterton, Penty, and Taylor attended early Fabian Society meetings (before its collectivism drove them away); contributed to the "socialist" *New Age* that A. R. Orage purchased from Catholic trade unionist Joseph Clayton in 1907 (soon after which it *dropped* "socialist" from its masthead); and chaired an occasional meeting of the Church Socialist League, which maintained that "all social questions should be studied in the light of Christian theology."† Loose participation in these circles helped – for instance – Belloc to elaborate the Servile State (years before his book would appear) and champion the Catholic vision of widely distributed property ownership in, e.g., the following terms:

> The criticism I offer to collectivism is offered by the whole weight and mass of Catholic opinion; in other words, it is the criticism offered by all that is healthy and permanent in the intellectual life of Europe; it is a criticism which has been repeated a hundred times in the French Parliament, and a thousand times in the Irish pulpits throughout the world. The sentiment of property

---

* See Gary Taylor, *Orage and the New Age* (Sheffield: Sheffield Hallam University, 2000) and *Socialism and Christianity: The Politics of the Church Socialist League* (Sheffield: Sheffield Hallam University, 2000); Niles Carpenter, *Guild Socialism* (New York: D. Appleton and Co., 1922); S. T. Glass, *The Responsible Society* (London, et al: Longmans, Green, and Co., 1966), Wallace Martin, *The New Age Under Orage* (Manchester: Manchester University Press, 1967), and Pius XI, *QA* §113–5. Cathrein highlights "orthodox" socialism's hostility to religion on pp. 205–8 of his work.

† *Socialism and Christianity*, p. 1.

is normal to and necessary to a citizen. Exactly the same thing as makes Catholic opinion as a whole today, and Catholic countries in the past, the enemies of the rich, of landlordism, and the rest, exactly the same instinct which in the Middle Ages gave every man capital, forced it on him as it were; exactly the same self-preserving sense as made Catholic societies reject the beastly economies of industrialism in its beginnings; in a word, the moral health which, after a century of industrialism, leaves the Catholic the only healthy soldier in Western Europe, makes him perceive that the divorce of personality from production is inhuman, and of itself just as inhuman when it is effected by collectivism with a charitable object as when it is effected by the present industrial system with an immoral and selfish object.*

The candor of the early 1900's gives us Belloc at his Catholic best in *The New Age* and Stirling Taylor's *Guild State*, based upon his conversations with Penty who, though not Catholic, thought himself Thomist and anti-Protestant. It is a testament to the Catholic idea that it is defended even by non-Catholic men of sense and vision. Penty, Taylor, Massingham, and Reckitt (who wisely called for a clean break of the guild movement from socialism†) are prime English examples, as are the "Christian Socialists" of 1848 who did *not* demand the abolition of private property (the essence of socialism, as Fr. Cathrein says) but sought "privileges of ownership [for] the propertyless worker."‡ Even Orage sought a "value beyond life" to establish social order, and, with Ramiro de Maeztu, T. E. Hulme, and J. M. Kennedy, fought relativism, modernism, and the resulting "twin rocks of shipwreck," liberalism and collectivism.§

---

* "Thoughts About Modern Thought," *The New Age*, Vol. II, No. 6, December 7, 1907, p. 108.

† *Socialism and Christianity*, p. 85.

‡ Gordon K. Lewis, "The Ideas of the Christian Socialists of 1848," *Western Political Quarterly*, Vol. 4, No. 3, Sep., 1951, p. 409. Joseph Clayton, reviewing Charles E. Raven's *Christian Socialism*, explains that during the Second Spring of English Catholicism "the Christian Socialists, whose antecedents [included] Carlyle, Coleridge, and Southey," were shocked by "the horrors perpetrated on men, women, and children by triumphant and unrestrained capitalism . . . ," and decided that "the Christian people of God must take their part against 'the unsocial Christians and the unchristian socialists'" (*Economics for Christians* (Oxford: Basil Blackwell, 1923, adapted from articles in *Blackfriars*, *The New Witness*, and *The Catholic Citizen*), pp. 74–5).

§ Martin, p. 218; see also his Chapters XI and XII, and Pius XI, *QA* §46.

There is "no possibility of an efficient stand against socialism from the side of liberalism," says Fr. Cathrein, for "the principles set up and defended by liberals logically lead to socialism . . . . " Among those he enumerates are atheism, materialism, "equality"; the labor theory of value of Smith, Ricardo, Say, and others; the centralization of state power; and its violent suppression of those "protecting organizations which . . . had arisen to counteract un-limited competition"; as a result, he says, " . . . society was disinte-grated, the weaker industries were isolated, and, owing to unlim-ited competition, fell victims to the superior power of capital."*

It is therefore impossible to remedy today's globalist collectiv-ism with yesterday's liberalism. Even the "guild socialist" alternative was welcomed by the Catholic Social Guild, "in so far as it is a return to those saner instincts of association that prevailed when Christendom was a reality."† How much more vital is the Catholic route sketched by Stirling Taylor, and confirmed by all of history:

> The conception that industry is best regulated upon a co-opera-tive model, and that such a model is most human and therefore best when the intimate human interests of each particular trade are expressed externally and politically by a Guild, to which is confided the conduct of that trade, is as old as civilisation.‡

Belloc also warned that the restoration of regulative guilds of property-owning men "does presuppose a sort of revolution of men's souls," but "[w]here men still have the virility to demand Property it can and has been accomplished."§ Let G. R. S. Taylor inspire us, then, to undertake at least the beginnings of that revo-lution, culminating in the foundation of a second Christendom.

The Directors, IHS Press
June 2, 2006
Feast of the Sacred Heart of Jesus

---

* *Socialism*, pp. 223–4, 230–32.

† Francis Goldwell, *Guild Socialism* (London: Catholic Social Guild, 1918), p. 37.

‡ Hilaire Belloc, "An Examination of the National Guild System," *The New Age*, Vol. XIII, No. 23, Oct. 2, 1913, p. 656.

§ *Ibid*, Vol. XIV, No. 5, Dec. 4, 1913, p. 140.

Foreword

ARLY IN THE TWENTIETH CENTURY, in Britain, a political movement emerged based on a remarkable combination of ideas which today might be labeled as both backward-looking and progressive. It included strains of many schools: romantic neo-medievalism, socialism, industrial unionism, syndicalism, and anarchism. However utopian (in some senses of that abused word), "guild socialism" was expressed and argued practically, and was deeply rooted in the England of the period just after World War I. It is such a distinctive social theory that it deserves continued study and still has lessons to teach. Relatively localist in orientation, guild socialism was (among other things) a reaction to the beginning of globalization in the 1890's, and to the global conflict that followed it. Living, as we do, in a period of hyper-global-ization and rising conflict, when state socialism seems clearly not a viable alternative and capitalism's dark side is more and more in evidence, we may share the concern of the guild socialists to maintain the vitality of local organization.

Considering its dual roots in radical labor agitation and backward-looking neo-medievalism, it cannot be surprising that the Guild movement contained tendencies that pulled in opposite directions. The consensus position of the Guildsmen was that functional organization by branch of production, that is, guild organization, was to be found in many past societies. Indeed, this form of organization could be seen as more natural than the modern system of politics based on territory and economics based on property. Thus, the Guild program could be seen not as the creation of a new society, but as the restoration of a kind of society that had been fairly well realized at some former time, such as medieval Europe or classical Greece.

Taylor's book is a strong statement for the "backward-looking" tendency of the Guild movement—one which diverged from the "guild socialism" proper of Hobson and Cole's National Guilds. Guildsmen in general were divided on the role of the state. Under the influence of the syndicalist (or frankly anarcho-syndicalist) and anarchist movements, some argued that the federation of the guilds should entirely replace the state. Others, Taylor among them, reserved a special role for the state even in a fully developed Guild society. The conflict between these two views accounts for some of the notorious complexity of G. D. H. Cole's proposals in *Guild Socialism Restated* (New Brunswick, N.J.: Transaction Books, 1980; first published 1920).

Taylor's view on this is perhaps his most distinctive point, separating him and other "neo-medievalists" from the main current of guild socialism. Among the functions he reserves to the state are the chartering of guilds; he proposes that the charters have a time limit and might impose on the guilds, along with other regulatory norms, the requirement of a rent as compensation for their use of the resources of society in production.

If taken as strict history, Taylor's vision of the medieval period would be somewhat misleading, because his sketch is limited to the cities, where only a small proportion of medieval Europeans lived. And it is specifically the medieval city that he brings up again and again as a contrast to the modern city: "it is the man who says that Birmingham is a greater city than Bruges who is giddy with sentiment" (*The Guild State*, p. 118). But it is, of course, the medieval city that can be defended as a precedent for the Guild idea. Whereas the medieval city was small by the standards of modern cities, usually better called a town, it was large enough for a considerable differentiation of function, without which functional organization is meaningless. Taylor might have said that guild organization is the natural way for cities, and might then have argued that guild-like organization is more important than ever, because industrialization has brought the vast majority of modern populations into urban conditions, by contrast with the Middle Ages.

Medieval society had a property that modern society lacks, a property rather like the forms of fractal geometry: fractal forms look similar when viewed at very different scales. We see this in medieval society also. In the medieval cities, the guild is a voluntary association of persons for mutual and common benefit; the city in turn is (ideally) a voluntary association of guilds for mutual and common benefit, and the Hansa or other league is a voluntary association of cities for mutual and common benefit. In some cases this is also seen at the territorial level, where for example the city of Siena is an association of Contrati that are themselves associations of neighbors. Even in the rural society we see something of this same independence of scale as the relation of villager to Lord (however undemocratic!) resembles the relationship of Lord to Duke, Duke to King, and indeed King to Emperor or Pope.

By contrast, modern societies do not have this property of independence of scale. The larger units, national states, are composed quite differently than the smaller units within them. The national states claim an absolute sovereignty based not on association but on a constitution, written or unwritten, and mutable only in small ways and under extraordinary circumstances. Absolute sovereignty demands fixed boundaries, and so the boundaries effectively have constitutional status. In the most extreme form there is no constituent part of a state except the individual and his property. This extreme is modified in practice by federalism in some cases, by the existence of business corporations, and by the increasingly recognized importance of "civil society" composed of voluntary organizations. But those parts do not (except for federalism) constitute the national state, nor are they constituted in similar ways. In federalism, the federal states may in theory constitute the national state, but in practice it is merely that their boundaries and distinctions attain constitutional status along with the boundaries of the national state.

The notorious vagueness of territorial boundaries in medieval times (*The Guild State,* Chapter I) follows from this property of independence of scale. Since the larger units are composed as the smaller units are, and are equally mutable, there are no uncontingent boundaries among them. At the same time, there is no barrier to a wider, more inclusive unity, however symbolic it may be. The co-operative movement had also envisioned a society with such a property of independence of scale. In the co-operative economic system they envisioned, the local workers' and consumers' co-operatives would be voluntary associations of persons, for mutual and common benefit, and would then form themselves into co-operative associations of co-operatives, for mutual and common benefit, which would ultimately assume the task of managing the economy. For the anti-state wing of Guild thinkers, this common vision, uniting the medieval city and the nineteenth-century working class co-operative, is the key. They had the same idea, elaborated it, and extended it to propose that the co-operative associations of co-operatives would themselves, largely if not entirely, constitute the state.

G.R.Stirling Taylor's work does not resolve the tension between medievalism and progressivism in the Guild movement, but that tension perhaps was not and is not to be resolved. It is this creative tension that gives the history of guild socialism, and that of related thinkers, its continuing interest. At any rate, Taylor's work is useful as a view into the world of the Guildsmen from a particular time and perspective, with a distinctive view of the relationship of local democracy to political authority. And if his vision can give us an alternative answer to the question of how to maintain local initiative and economic democracy in everyday life in the face of increasing global interdependence, it will be well worth study.

Roger McCain, Ph.D.
Professor, Economics and International Business
Drexel University, Philadelphia, Pennsylvania
June 29, 2006
Feast of Ss. Peter and Paul

INTRODUCTION
Guilds and the Faith

N 1871 JOHN RUSKIN BEGAN a series of *Letters to the Workmen and Labourers of Great Britain,* which were to run into four volumes, published under the title *Fors Clavigera.** In these letters Ruskin proposed the establishment of a "Guild of St. George," which would directly and actively oppose industrialism and its waste of lives and resources. By placing his guild under the patronage of St. George, Ruskin intended to focus attention on the Christian *ethos* in which the social good was held superior to individual greed.† Whilst Ruskin's Christian faith, in the sense of *Credo*—"I believe"—was, to say the least, somewhat eccentric, it is beyond dispute that his values and ethics were of a high Christian morality. It might be said that whatever his deism, he was an "ethical Christian" and one of the noblest minds in English history. It was from Ruskin and the "Guild of St. George" that William Morris and others drew their inspiration.

The development of Ruskin's teachings by his disciples after 1906, however, certainly seems to have been away from any explicit Christian ethos, as was later to become apparent with the defection of Palme Dutt, William Gallagher, and Maurice Dobb, among others, to the newly founded Communist Party of Great Britain. After an unsuccessful attempt to take over the Fabian Society, the "guild socialists" established their own National Guilds League.

---

* Vol. 1 (London: George Allen, 1899); especially the unpaginated "advice to the new edition."

† See Janet Barnes, *St. George, Ruskin and the Dragon* (Sheffield: Ruskin Gallery, 1992), p. 9.

William Titterton described the guild approach to industrialism:

> [I]t proved the virtue, the necessity, of organization from the productive unit, the master-craftsman, outwards, instead of organizing inwards from the consuming unit, conceived by the Fabians as the nation, if not the world.*

However this very high degree of organization, which has something of the ethos of Bellamy's *Looking Backward*† about it, was the cause of division. S.G.Hobson developed a more moderate programme and had the support of A.R.Orage and the influential *New Age*. It was their proposed organization of all workers in a given occupation into a single guild – which would therefore have a monopoly of both labour and capital – which G.R.Stirling Taylor and A.J.Penty rejected. It might be convenient to distinguish here between the two schools of thought, reserving the term "guild socialism" for the "organization" men and "guildism" for the decentralists, with the proviso that the division was neither clear-cut nor hard and fast. In *The Guild State*, Stirling Taylor offered a pragmatic, trial-and-error approach, concluding his preface with the words: "Their interpretation owes more to the teaching of everyday life than to the professors."

The guilds must not, he maintains, begin with a "blue-print," a mass of regulations, caveats, and codicils, but develop organically by testing what works and rejecting what does not. They are not, in fact, a "new" thing, rather they have their roots in custom, in a tradition, and it is this tradition which calls men back to their roots – and what can be more radical than that? This view of society is one which echoes Chesterton's defence of tradition in *Orthodoxy* as "the proxy of the dead and the enfranchisement of the unborn." In contrast to the guild-socialist aim of "National" Guilds, Stirling Taylor proposes, on the medieval model, "local" guilds, which may be municipal or even operate in a single ward; which may have a

---

* *G. K. Chesterton: A Portrait* (London: Douglas Organ, 1947), p. 63.
† See the review of *Looking Backward* by William Morris in *Commonweal*, June 22, 1889, in A. L. Morton, ed., *Political Writings of William Morris* (London: Lawrence & Wishart, 1984).

hundred members or only a dozen; which may compete with each other, moderately, and leave choice to the customer. In comparing the author's proposals with the social teaching of the Catholic Church it must be remembered that the economy of truth requires that the Church defines the *minimum* of doctrine, leaving much open to exegesis. It is in the Catholic *ethos* that we will find the larger concordance with "guildism," rather than in the body of defined doctrine. On the issue of subsidiarity, however, we find Stirling Taylor at one with the authoritative, and subsequent, teaching of Pius XI in his 1931 *Quadragesimo Anno:*

> The supreme authority of the State ought, therefore, to let subordinate groups handle matters and concerns of lesser importance, which would otherwise dissipate its efforts greatly. Thereby the State will more freely, powerfully, and effectively do all those things that belong to it alone . . . (§80).
> The social policy of the State, therefore, must devote itself to the re-establishment of the Industries and Professions (§82).

Pius XI continues his exposition of the nature and purpose of such associations in the clearest terms, which might indeed have been suggested by *The Guild State.* The bonds which claim the allegiance of men, the encyclical asserts, are not forged by their position in the labour-market, but by their being united in the functions they exercise in society:

> For it is natural that just as those who dwell in close proximity constitute townships, so those who practice the same trade or profession, in the economic field or any other, form corporate groups. These groups, with powers of self-government, are considered by many to be, if not essential to civil society, at least natural to it (§83).

It would not be too strong to say that Taylor and Penty were confidently proposing a Catholic alternative to the secularist view of the guild socialists. I say "confidently" because Belloc, one of the founders of Distributism, which is clearly inherent in Taylor's decentralist proposals, had given Catholics a new and assertive confidence in their roots and in their past. He had called the modern world before the bar of history, and found it wanting. He had proclaimed to his fellow Catholics that they "mistook the hour of the day. It is not the night, it is the dawn." Taylor and Penty, thanks to Belloc, were certain that the Catholic ages had done things better and to these they proposed a return, not in detail, but in spirit.

Ruskin, in *Unto This Last,* had demolished, in scintillating prose, the "iron laws" of that "common or garden political economist," who leaves out of the equation the most vital element – human affections. The just master, who is considerate of his workmen and of their re-creation, will always be given more, better, and more willing service than the harsh taskmaster who adheres to the so-called "iron laws" of rent and wages. In the same way some of the guild socialists, chiefly those who defected to communism, left out of account the social ethic without which the National Guilds would wither and die – as indeed they did. This might perhaps be illustrated with a simple example.

A cricket (or baseball) club is founded on an ethic, which we term "sportsmanship." The components of this ethic cannot be disentangled from the whole, and they certainly cannot be exhaustively subjected to "laws," a point Stirling Taylor makes concerning the guilds and the state. In fact, in a sport such as cricket or baseball, the "laws" will rarely be changed, nor will the match be stopped every few minutes whilst the players argue about the laws and demand changes – that would be contrary to the ethic of sportsmanship. A player may know all the rules of the game and be master of all the skills it requires, but if he lacks the ethic he will be a cheat and bring dishonour on the club. If we apply this model to the guilds and their place in the wider society, we will see immediately, as Stirling Taylor saw, that the guilds can only flourish, or indeed exist as guilds and not as the petrifacts of a by-gone age, in a society governed, not by regulations, but by an ethic, a sixth sense which tells a man what he *may* do, what he may *not* do, and what he *ought* to do. For the medieval guilds that ethic was Catholic Christianity, and the whole guild socialist attempt to do without it ended in failure.

It is plain from the text that Stirling Taylor rejects the notion of "common ownership" adopted by the National Guilds League in favour of the Distributist (and medieval) concept of ownership of workshop and tools by the master craftsmen, their families, journeymen, and apprentices, associating in a guild. In this he is at one with Leo XIII's defence of private property in *Rerum Novarum* (1891):

> We have seen that this great labour question cannot be solved save by assuming as a principle that private ownership must be held sacred and inviolable. The law, therefore, should favour ownership, and its policy should be to induce as many as possible of the people to become owners . . . (§46).
> Men always work harder and more readily when they work on that which belongs to them; nay, they learn to love the very soil that yields in response to the labour of their hands, not only food to eat, but an abundance of good things for themselves and those that are dear to them . . . . These . . . important benefits, however, can be reckoned on only provided that a man's means be not drained and exhausted by excessive taxation. The right to possess private property is derived from nature, not from man; and the State has the right to control its use in the interests of the public good alone, but by no means to absorb it altogether (§47).

Penty's "guildism" and Distributism met in the pages of Orage's *New Age* where they were later to be joined by Douglas' Social Credit. There were, as already mentioned, very profound disputes. Orage, for example, declared himself a "Distributist," even though he concurred in the centralization of organization implicit in National Guilds and was prepared to accept the factory system. Penty and Chesterton on the other hand looked for the end of the factory system and the decentralization of production. Belloc, whilst championing ownership also saw a role for the guilds as complementing private property with cooperation.*

Distributism was associated with, and perhaps even part of, the wider "back to the land" movement. One result of this was that Distributists, typified by Titterton, tended to think of "property"

---

* See *The Chesterton Review*, Vol. I., No. 2, Spring-Summer, 1975, p. 55.

as ownership of land. They overlooked the fact that, for example, a practice such as a doctor, dentist, solicitor, architect, etc. is "property," albeit abstract property, even if conducted from rented premises. So also might be a workshop or factory owned by, as Stirling Taylor suggests, a guild of common function.

With the meeting of these three strands in the pages of *The New Age*, and later in *G. K.'s Weekly*, "social Thomism" was brought back to life and into the twentieth century.

> It was St. Thomas's argument for social self-sufficiency, as explained in *De Regimine Principium*, that convinced Penty of the supreme necessity of getting away from an industrial commercial society. Aquinas decried the growth of "cosmopolitanism," "as detrimental to fostering a stable life based on one's own social environment." . . . Penty's entire philosophy came very close to one of the strongest traditions of Catholic social thinking, namely, the emphasis on the efficacy of the self-contained organic community.[*]

There was of course, as already touched upon, disputation, for all these men were original thinkers, not likely to follow-my-leader meekly or mouth the unthinking slogans of conventional wisdom. Belloc grasped Douglas's theorem as quickly as Orage. Indeed he illustrated it more clearly than Douglas himself:

> Industrial Capitalism has broken down because it is producing an amount of wealth greater than it is distributing purchasing power for that wealth; and to put it very crudely indeed, if I want to make a hundred thousand boots, or rather employ men to make those boots, and by the time the boots are made I have distributed to the men who make them the money wherewith to purchase thirty-thousand boots, what am I to do with the seventy thousand boots left?[†]

---

[*] J. P. Corrin, "The Formation of the Distributist Circle," *ibid.*, p. 61. [The work of St. Thomas referenced is actually *De Regno.*—Ed.]
[†] Hilaire Belloc, address of May 26, 1933, *G. K.'s Weekly*, June 8, 1933.

Belloc did not dispute the correctness of the Douglas theorem, but he regarded it as of less importance than the distribution of ownership. He overlooked what the late Canon Drinkwater pointed out in *Why Not End Poverty?*—that given security of income by the national dividend, men would in fact be able to buy property.

Douglas in turn approved Orage's guild socialism, seeing a first step towards it in the shop steward movement. He took the view that the Social Credit proposals for honest money and just prices were the practical mechanism for achieving Distributism.

> It is profoundly significant that what is now called "Socialism," and pretends to be a movement for the improvement of the underprivileged, began as something closely approaching the Distributism of Messrs. Belloc and Chesterton, of which the financial proposals embodied in various authentic Social Credit Schemes form the practical mechanism.... It (Socialism) was penetrated by various subversive bodies and perverted into the exact opposite of Distributism: Collectivism.*

Titterton never fully accepted that Orage was a "real" Distributist because he accepted the factory system as permanent; but why should not factories be owned by syndicates of those who work in them, or better still, by guilds founded upon shared function, as Stirling Taylor advocates?

Maurice Reckitt, convinced alike of Distributism and the correctness of the Douglas theorem, worked hard—though without success—for a synthesis of all three strands.

What would that synthesis be? It would embody the Catholic teaching on property, its inalienable rights and corresponding duties. It would embrace, through Stirling Taylor's and Penty's "guildism," the Church's teaching on cooperation between classes by unifying those sharing the same economic function. It would give us the just price, so long the subject of theological examination, and it would give us honest money, safeguarded from loss of value (i.e., theft) from both inflation and deflation.

---

* C. H. Douglas, *The Social Creditor,* January 16, 1943.

23

Stirling Taylor's prose is calm and stately, often Bellocian in its insights and dismissals. I have hinted already that there are passages in Pius XI's encyclical which echo his thought. I have not discussed the organizational details of the guilds for the good reason that Stirling Taylor himself appears to consider them as secondary to the spirit of the guilds, which must be guided by the Church and the Holy Ghost if it is to triumph. His ideas must be maintained against the time when industrialism and usury implode for lack of the very resources which they have wasted.

I have endeavoured to reflect the Catholic-Distributist ethos of *The Guild State* without resorting to extensive quotations from the text, for that, after all, is what you will be reading next.

Anthony Cooney
Liverpool, England
July 2, 2006
Feast of the Visitation of the Blessed Virgin Mary

THE WEAVERS' HALL
THE COOMBE, DUBLIN

PREFACE

N THE SOCIAL BAROMETER the needle shows threatening signs of finding the markings on the dial too few to register its lowest intentions. There is consequently much hurrying to and fro in the world–like a camp scuttling to tighten the ropes before the wind begins. The soldiers and the politicians, knowing little of history–or anything else–vainly imagined that they could give us their Great Plague of 1914–1918, and that no Wat Tylers[1] and John Balls[2] would arise hereafter to declare that they disliked the results. Today, the rulers of the earth probably realize that they have been like schoolboys recklessly playing in a powder magazine. Hence a sudden crop of books on reform and reconstruction, as numberless as the good intentions with which the other world is rumoured to be already paved. They would be admirable books, so many of them, if it were not for the somewhat vital defect that they ignore most of the facts. More especially, they refuse to take man–that patient sport of the wits and the wise–as he really exists, but rather as a dummy studio model, which they may dress according to their weirdest tastes. There was once, it is said, a learned professor who set himself to write an essay on the giraffe. He did not go to Africa to see one; he retired to a tower and wrote a beautiful and convincing book out of his imagination.

The following essay is an attempt to state the guild remedy for the disasters of modern statesmanship. It is based on dull facts and the most commonsense deductions therefrom. It takes man as he is; and history as he has made it. It has therefore little to do with the mankind that politicians dream of, or with the history that historians write.

In a world submerged in the sentimental rhetoric of cabinet ministers and newspaper writers, and the Myrtle Villa[3] ideals of the suburbs they so fittingly represent, one clings rather eagerly to the hope of better things. The eye catches some notes just written by Mr. Paton,[4] the new organizing secretary of the National Guilds League. He is moved to joy that while Watt[5] was toiling to invent the steam engine, "a few miles down the river, at Poosie Nancy's[6] cheerful board, a greater than Watt, commanding mightier forces still, caroused with his boon companions"; and when this secretary in the labour movement, skilled in the knowledge of trade union rules, goes on to ask whether the author of the machine industry deserves "honour or execration," then there is hope that the workers will be taught real economics at last; and, incidentally, that the "educated" will be taught good taste.

The facts on which this book is based are drawn from the standard historical and economic sources, too numerous to name. Their interpretation owes more to the teaching of everyday life than to the professors; though this essay would probably not have been attempted but for the advantage of many conversations with Mrs. Emily Townshend[7] and Mr. Arthur Penty.[8]

G. R. S. T.

THE SEAL OF THE DUBLIN GUILD
OF BARBER-SURGEONS

THE GUILD STATE

CHAPTER I

THE HISTORICAL BASIS OF
THE GUILD SYSTEM

THERE IS A FANTASTIC RUMOUR, circulating in the main among historical dons and in political clubs, that progress is the discovery of something new. Whereas, in truth, it is far more often the return to something old. One looks in baffled search for the origin of this most amazing error; for it is without proof either in the records of the past or in the facts of the present. The historians and the politicians have seemingly made an unpardonable mistake; which, fortunately, that sane creature, the normal healthy man, has not shared with them. For the common people are not so easily lured into the quicksands of loose thinking as are those who spend their lives in libraries and parliament chambers. It has been the rarest of events when the people have asked for new laws: in their times of revolt they have so persistently desired that they should return to something already possessed in the past. When William the Conqueror[9] intruded himself into our social system, his subjects (being somewhat troubled by his "higher" civilization) could think of nothing more to their minds than a return to the customs of the Confessor; a request which they continued to make until the new Norman laws had become old enough to be bearable. The Great Charter of John[10] was really a poor thing in any democratic sense, for it said so little about anyone except the barons; yet it was

popular – probably because it contained very little that was new. A few hundred years afterwards, when the growth of the politicians' new parliamentary system was obviously sapping the liberty of the people, there arose a cry for reform – Englishmen began to demand again the liberties of the Feudal Ages, as written in John's charter. However, this is not a history book; what one desires here is to recall the historical fact that common men rarely ask for anything new in their social structure. They have a stubborn belief that the old ways are better.

It is remarkable that so many people are asking today for some explanation of the guild system, for the guilds are not a new idea. They are, on the contrary, probably the most widely spread idea on the earth, and one of the very oldest. In asking for a guild system, one is not asking for anything new, but for something exceedingly old. This is not another of those new-fangled notions of political circles, but something so old and well established in the history of the world that the politicians have never heard of it. For a long part of the history of mankind, the guilds have been an essential element in almost all societies. Since men first became craftsmen and industrialists, instead of nomads and cave-dwellers, the almost universal judgement of mankind has accepted the guild system as the most rational manner in which the work of the world can most easily be done. This is not the place to offer proofs of that statement; they are to be found in the whole of history, and concerning almost every people under the sun. In India, China, Greece, Rome; in all Europe since it gave up barbarism; in the whole world even before it became quite civilized – as police court magistrates understand that term – the guilds have had a universal place. But it was in those days which we now collect together under the name of the "Middle Ages" that the guilds reached their prime. During the thirteenth and fourteenth centuries the guilds ranked in Western Europe with the barons and the kings, as the dominant factors in the social structure of their period.

The observer in England today can so easily lose a sense of proportion in judging the guild idea; he thinks of it as past and somewhat local, while with equal ease he imagines that our present economic system is universal; whereas it is only local even today. In the pages of history, modern capitalism is a mere novelty, an upstart theory without a pedigree – and perhaps without a future. It is all-important to start our analysis with a proper sense of proportion between the old and the new; it will restore that due balance of the mind which the insistent shriek of "the new" in every morning paper so unconsciously tends to overturn.

It must not be forgotten that the guild system even at its prime was only one part of a greater whole. That great adventure of man which we tell as the tale of the Middle Ages; that very subtle blending of mind and matter, of spirit and craft, which we call the medieval social system, was the whole which we must realize if we are to understand the guilds, which are only a part of it. For they are not something which can be torn from its setting, as a jewel can be dislodged from a ring. They were too organic a part of the medieval age to survive such an outrage. The sceptics are right when they continually chatter in our ears: "You cannot go back" – if they mean that it is impossible to tear a part from the old, in the vain hope of fitting it into a new system that is as the Pole from the Pole apart. When we understand a little of what the Middle Ages were, then we may know what the guilds meant in a social system which they did so much to build.

It was written above that the guilds ranked with the kings and the barons as the foundation of medieval society. But strictly speaking the king, although the centre of the picture, was less important in detail than the other two; and by understanding why we shall understand also that main principle of medievalism – local independence – on which the guilds themselves depended, and must always depend – for it is the root principle of their existence.

The king and his law are almost modern ideas, and certainly as we know them both today, would have been entirely beyond the conception of a medieval mind. We think of the king as the symbol of a great central government, imposing his law on his subjects by all the majesty of the police, from the Lord Chancellor to the village constable. When the guilds were alive, their members would have found it difficult to grasp any such idea. The king was to them a faraway creature whose main function was to lead the nation in war and defend it from attack. It was certainly not his function to interfere as a legislator or judge in their private affairs, which they felt quite capable of managing themselves. Parliament, insofar as it was a fact at all, they regarded as a body of representatives sent to Westminster to make as good a bargain as possible in the matter of taxation; and then return home again as quickly as possible and get to their honest work. Scarcely anyone would have thought of Parliament as an institution to make "laws."

"Law" was a rare event in the history of the Middle Ages; and kings were people of modest claims. The medieval man governed himself in a democratic sense which seems beyond the realms of fantasy in these despotic days of universal suffrage and innumerable popular councils. Instead of electing delegates to make laws at Westminster, the people of the Middle Ages were their own legislators at home. It may sound very rural; but we have failed to grasp the fact that it is really far better to be so safe in our freedom that we do not need to be protected by representatives at all. It is only necessary to send our man to Parliament when we have reason to believe that somebody there is going to take away our rights. But in the Middle Ages there was so little intrusion of that sort by autocratic gentlemen at Westminster. Indeed, they had scarcely invented that impertinent thing we now call "government."

The origin of our Parliament is a case in point. It was not any desire of the people that created it. It never entered their heads that somebody at Westminster should make laws for Somerset or Yorkshire. Parliaments began because the Crown had, in some way or another, to persuade the people to be taxed. It was only as an afterthought that the members of the House of Commons thought that, if they had to pay, it would be as well to get something in return. So they asked for laws – not laws to tell the people what they must do, but mainly to tell the king what he must not do. However, the kings also saw their chance, and they soon invented the autocratic, compelling "law" which we know today. But that was not an idea of the Middle Ages, and when it was invented, and imposed, then the medieval system rapidly disappeared. For the very heart of it was that the people had to an extraordinary degree the liberty to make their own law and order. That is a historical fact, which some people imagine a mere light-hearted paradox–but that is because they know very little about history.

The compelling force of the Middle Ages was not law, but custom. One has said that the people made their own laws at home; but the statement requires instant qualification. For they can scarcely be said to have "made" laws at all. They did not vote new rules. They rather lived after the traditions which their fathers had handed down to them; for men that possess the traditions of centuries have little need for the laws of yesterday or today. For tradition is the everlasting memory of mankind; remembering the great lessons of its past, storing them up in the mind of man, until they become instinctive, even as the half-conscious knowledge of the beast is stored as a protection from danger.

The government of the Middle Ages, such as it existed at all, was almost purely local. The great modern state was unknown. There was certainly a man who called himself King of England, and one who called himself King of the French; but compared with the kings and presidents of today, they were mere babes at the game of ruling: they were far too gentlemanly to think of anything so crude and unmannerly. The government was accomplished by manorial courts, and burgesses of the towns; abbots in their mon-asteries, and barons in their castles, were the factors of public life with which they reckoned in those days, in a much deeper sense than they reckoned with the king. Kent did not much mind what they were doing in Warwickshire, and would certainly have resent-ed it keenly if Warwickshire men had been too inquisitive about Kent. That very exaggerated social factor, rather cleverly termed "public business," had then scarcely been invented. (Now that it has arrived as a much-extolled social function, it is interesting to notice that so much of it is still mainly the private business of the councillors and their personal friends, and has comparatively little to do with the interest of their constituents. But the disadvantages of central government will be discussed later.) Private business, in its more legitimate sense, was good enough for the wise creatures of the Middle Ages. Their main business was doing their daily work; and they were not over-anxious about what was happening somewhere else. In earlier days, even the murder of one's neighbour to a large extent was private business, which mainly concerned the two families of the victor and the victim. Such public business as there was had rather the air of the parish council than of the more pompous Houses of Parliament; it was a question for a guild regulation, a municipal or manorial custom. They never discussed the best method of conquering the other ends of the earth, and rarely even discussed a constitution for their own country. Government dealt with homely facts, not with faraway theories.

Since there were in those days such shadowy great nations and such small governing units, it is not surprising that government was so local an institution. National affairs had not been found necessary, because there were scarcely any nations. They are only a modern idea. We read of the mighty struggle between Athens and Sparta; and perhaps picture it in terms of two states as we know them today. We forget that they were neighbouring towns, about forty miles apart as the crow flew. It was as if Birmingham had challenged Manchester to mortal combat. The moral for the moment is that in the Middle Ages towns were as important as great states today, not that they were as trivial as modern towns. The Middle Ages built up a gorgeous structure of intellect and economics and art on a basis that knew nothing of such a modern notion as an empire.

Here we are faced with a grave exception; and it is the exception which may help to prove the rule. The Catholic Church of Rome claimed that it gathered under its guiding hand the whole sweep of the world of Western Europe. It deliberately, in the very heyday of the medieval ideals, conceived of the great society of the Holy Roman Church. Now the essence of the modern great state is that it is based on the idea of coercion of arms, and maintained by the compulsion of magistrates and policemen and prison warders. Note how far away all this was from the ecclesiastical claims. The Catholic Church, in the theory of the Middle Ages, refused to sanction the shedding of blood. If it was to build itself a great state it must be by moral persuasion. It could excommunicate the sinner; it could not hang him. The Inquisition and the War of the Waldenses[11] were the practical and mainly local lapses of man from his theory, but if we are to make history the record of lapses, then indeed it will be a thing without form. If the Catholic Church had won its great contest with the emperors, then it is possible that we might have escaped this nightmare of great autocratic nations, tearing out each other's vitals. Europe might well be now governed by a moral force which had banished the crudity of physical force from civilization; and without physical force there could be no "nationalism" as we know it today. The nationalism of races will survive, as the individuality of individuals will survive in a reasonable society; but it will not be that artificial thing, the "nationality" which has grown round the ambitions of kings and their bureaucrats. The victory of the Church of Rome would have been the defeat of physical tyranny, and it was the physical tyranny of the armies of autocratic kings that broke the local freedom of the Middle Ages as a martyr was broken on the wheel. But it was the bureaucrat and the politician – not the king so much – who reaped the fruits of that conquest.

It is natural that in this medieval society of commonsense people the guilds should take a supremely important part. In an age when government was both local and economic, instead of centralized and political – that is, when the town or village mainly ruled itself, and when its "laws" were the rules of everyday business affairs – then the guild, being the collective assembly of the local wisdom and business experience, naturally took a foremost place in public life. If the king did endeavour to interfere in local government, for a long time it was merely to acknowledge by his approval the laws which the local assemblies had already acknowledged for themselves. It was merely a tactful courtesy on the part of the local councils. Thus the king would grant a charter recognizing the customs of the burgesses of a town or the members of a guild. They were rarely new laws; they were those that were already obeyed. Slowly the central powers built up a governing hierarchy of their own: the sheriffs, the justices of the King's

Court, the lord-lieutenants of the counties, gradually sucked the power from the local assemblies and held it in the hands of the councils and officers of the Crown. But when that was accomplished, the Middle Ages were no more; the modern system had begun. In medieval days government was, in the main, the laws of town council and guild. It was a matter of the serious practical affairs of everyday life – not the discussion of vague sentimentalities, which newspaper editors now call "politics." And of this very practical businesslike medieval society, the guilds were the most substantial foundation – while the kings and their parliaments were the gay flags and gilded weathercocks which gave colour and sparkle to the show – and have confused the childlike minds of the orthodox historical dons ever since.

There are those who will say that this theory of the Middle Ages is a pleasant dream for the idealists. But there is really no need to leave the discussion in the field of vague theory. The period can be approached as a fact. Let us agree to differ as to what the medieval men possessed in the way of a political or social constitution; let us doubt all their ideals; let us dismiss medievalism as a dream of the "modern romantic imagination." But there are certain survivals of the Middle Ages which cannot be so airily dismissed. It requires more imagination to dismiss Chartres Cathedral and Westminster Abbey than to accept them. We may argue that we do not like the thousands of medieval facts that are still dotted over Western Europe, in its churches and sculptures and manuscripts, but they cannot be flicked away by that phrase "romantic imagination." There are few with sufficient intellectual nerve to deny that the medieval constitution produced a very great architecture, sculpture, painting, literature, and philosophy of life, against which the products of modern society seem too often the refuse of a rummage sale. If we intend to prove that the modern system is better than the medieval system, then we must bravely face our task. We must prove, for example, that Manchester is better than Bruges, that Chicago is better than Florence. We must work out with some accuracy of detail that Mr. Churchill[12] is a greater statesman than St. Anselm,[13] and that

Lord Curzon[14] is a nobler figure than Simon de Montfort.[15] These are not questions that can be avoided in a maze of generalities and theories. They are facts, which are the very foundation of the argument.

But this is not the place either for argument or for proofs. It is now merely attempted to suggest in outline what it would need a hundred history books to prove. But whether we like its beauty and sanity or not, the Medieval Age in its main features had a symmetry of order which very clearly distinguishes it from the social order, or disorder, that governs us today. It was a system that knew little of the "laws" and political ideas that are the commonplaces of our public life now. The medieval man would have regarded the new kingdom, governed by a new king, and still newer bureaucrats, as an inconceivable monstrosity. The king and his central coercion were the mere surface of the Middle Ages; and in spite of the rudeness of barons and the turbulent vigour of a society which was not very regardful of life or of limb, yet, take it all in all, the Medieval Age was the time of a rough democratic liberty, a sound practical sense of what it was good for a king to do, and what it was none of his business to attempt.

There was no sudden change to the modern system, for there never is any sudden change in human affairs. There are political upheavals which the newspapers call "revolutions," but it is rarely that they dislodge more than a few stones in the fabric of social life. The Revolution is usually the device of a gang of political adventurers or police spies who see the opportunity to seize a little power – as less adventurous men snatch a leg of mutton from a butcher's stall. But as the snatching of mutton does not really disorganize the meat trade, so the scrambling of revolutionary adventurers scarcely shakes, except for a moment, the very steady fabric of humanity. It was no sudden upheaval that changed a medieval society into a modern one: it was an infinitely persistent undermining.

Whereas the medieval system was based on local production and local customs, and its civic organs were local and economic and democratic, the modern age is centralized, political and autocratic.

35

Expressed in material facts it is the difference between the city-states of Bruges or Florence and the massive Empire of Britain or the highly centralized Republic of France. There is one way in which this modern centralization can be quickly grasped. Take a historical atlas of medieval Europe. Note that after the break-up of the Roman Empire the broad masses of colour disappear from the maps: France, Germany, Italy, Spain, become a maze of small kingdoms and independent communes. Nations do not exist at the beginning of the period – though some of the Carolingian kings talked in big words of their rights and acres. Gradually the maps get simpler; fewer and fewer colours and boundary lines are needed to express the facts, for the counts and communes gradually gave place to greater kings and more comprehensive parliaments. For example, the seven kingdoms of the Heptarchy[16] give place to the one king at Winchester. Being only a king, of course he had little power in the Middle Ages, but he was the beginning of that process which was to end one day in this modern system of centralization, based on physical force and the intellectual tyranny which followed it. Only the Church of Rome emerged from the medieval debacle in the reverse order from the other great factors of the period; it came out, not more centralized, but split into many parts, perhaps because it alone did not base its rule on physical compulsion, which was the basis of all the powers of its companion potentates.

This centralization of governing power has been a slow process, and indeed, it is only in the last few decades that it has reached its full results in the breeding of an insolent plutocracy that resembles, with strange likeness, those vulgar rich who were bred by the like centralization which took place in the Roman Republic. For we must remember that Rome had already tried centralization centuries before Henry Tudor[17] and Louis XI[18] played that dangerous game in England and France. But could we live under their rule, it would seem like the Middle Ages to our modernized minds. If the modern system can be said to have a clear beginning, in the case of England it would certainly have to be placed in the time of the Tudor dynasty. Yet how far the end has gone beyond that beginning. Even the Tudors invented but a very few of the characteristics of the new system, or rather they were able to get only a few of its results. It needed much more than the drafting of a new constitution or the issue of a few official regulations to change the free citizens of the medieval community into the helpless tools of a modern state.

There are few things more characteristic of the modern system than one of its most characteristic products, the politicians. They are the keystone of the whole structure. Today they are thick as slugs after a summer rain, but in the Tudor period they had not yet been bred. Take the case of Queen Elizabeth;[19] she had perhaps the most honest and most efficient ministers of state that this nation has ever possessed. Burleigh[20] and Walsingham[21] thought of their country's welfare before their own; Walsingham did not even leave enough wealth to give his body a decent burial. It was certainly not the control of the House of Commons that kept such men straight; indeed, the Commons had not yet much power to exert. The governing machine was still compelled to use men who had not lost all sense of democratic needs and communal honour. Politics had not yet become a career by which one could win a fat post by serving the interests of the great merchants and bankers. It was not until much later that governing became a profession, and statesmen became politicians instead of administrators. Burleigh was a skilled administrator to his finger-tips, not a popular talker for use in the House of Commons. The state papers of his period are covered with his comments in his own handwriting, with careful summing of the arguments for and against. The modern politician scarcely ceases talking, while Burleigh rarely stopped working. He was almost everything that his successors are not. He is a summary of the vast change that has come over the art of government. We can trace its gradual decline in efficiency and honesty as the centralized system has developed, until today the word "politician" is a term of contempt.

Central government is the root of the modern system, and it includes within its scope affairs that were altogether outside the bounds of the medieval monarchy. The government now really tries to govern. Whether we call it Tory Democracy or Collectivist Socialism, the modern idea is that the people should receive their instructions from above. It is assumed that the state can govern its subjects far better than they can govern themselves. Perhaps if one can grasp the difference between the feudal Simon de Montfort and Mr. Lloyd George[22] one may get near the essential difference between the two systems. The object of the feudal lord was to free the English people from the control of a tyrannical state by taking away its powers. The aim of the modern politician appears to be to increase by every means that central power. The charters of the Plantagenet kings[23] were mainly to define what the Crown and its Council should not do. Today, the politician calls it "reform" when he adds to the power of the central government by piling an Insurance Act on the top of an Old Age Pension Act, and smothers them both with innumerable other acts for controlling the lives of the people down below. It is not necessary to criticize this as merely a matter of theory—for we are face to face with its appalling practical results.

That is the vital distinction between the old system and the new; it attempts to govern from the centre, instead of leaving it to the local parts. Since the Middle Ages there has been a continual weakening of the local power, and still more rapid growth of the central political organization. It is one of the great lessons of history—though few historians have learned it themselves, let alone taught it to their students—that the most inevitable result of this development is that government has ceased to be conducted by the men who are intimately in touch with the work in hand, and has passed into the control of the political amateurs and the clerical bureaucrats, who often have every qualification except personal knowledge of the work they are trying to manage. It is possible to concede that all our politicians will be saints and all our officials in Whitehall will be learned professors; yet modern government must sooner or later break down, because it is growing so complex and so remote from the facts of the case, that a sainted professor himself could not keep his head and heart in such a turmoil and confusion.

Government has come to be a massive structure in London, Paris, Berlin, Vienna, Petrograd and Rome. In these overstrained centres we find a vast crowd of officials who have but a trivial knowledge of what they ought to do, while outside are the passive citizens, who scarcely can discover what has been done. It is a tragedy of cross-purposes. It has become a superstition that this is the only way of governing, and that the only people who can do it are these politicians, with their bureaucrats and financial "advisers"–which seems the most discreet term for a somewhat delicately ambiguous relationship. But who started this superstition? The capitals of Europe are vastly important in the eyes of the people who write newspapers–but then it happens that these valuable journals are so often the property of the aforesaid ruling politicians themselves. Their newspaper bills announce that all the world is hanging by a fine thread on a decision of the Cabinet in Downing Street,[24] or the signing of a treaty in Paris. But the journalists are part owners, part servants in this great governing business; and when they cry the virtues of its wares, it is not very different from what appears in the next column, where a soap manufacturer advertises that his soap is the best in the world.

But the highest success of the modern system, as a piece of clever advertising, is the astounding statement that it is more democratic than the medieval system. A long list of franchise victories is displayed in every history book, showing how one class after another has been admitted to the mystic rites of the ballot box. Judging by the results so far, they might as well have been allowed to vote whether the aforesaid box should be painted black or white. The medieval man, without a vote, governed himself more freely than the citizen of the twentieth century, with his share in universal suffrage. The very slow-thinking historical dons have not yet discovered that the franchise is not a triumph of democracy, but another triumph–perhaps their greatest–for the political orators. Every name added to the electors' list has been another victim for the all-powerful centralized governors to fleece. This great Reform Act of 1918[25] has been the politicians' trump card: it added an odd six million voters to the list, and the nation promptly returned the largest number of plutocrats and political adventurers that England has seen. One prominent question was that of compulsory military service. There was scarcely a medieval monarch who would have dared to mention such a thing. A Plantagenet king once asked an earl to fight for him in France. The reply was scarcely fit for sensitive ears, though it so pleased the medievalists that it was given to the earl as a surname. No Stuart king, in his haughtiest moments, ever dared to claim a fraction of the power that living democratic cabinets assume as a matter of course. This pretence of democracy in the modern system is the greatest bluff in history.

Whereas the governing factors of the medieval system were something organically bound up with its life, being the almost spontaneous action of that life, in the modern period, on the contrary, government has become something much more external. It is the activity of the capital cities, not the work of the people. The central interference has great – and appalling – results; but it remains superficial, because it is not easy to change the nature of man from the outside. A government may change England from a pleasant land into a coal yard and a dustbin – which would seem to be the ideal of the present governing set – yet at heart these barbarians have changed very little. Take the case of France, perhaps the most highly centralized state in the world; yet the French peasant remains much as he has been for centuries – the most substantial fact in European civilization, and perhaps its highest product.

In spite of this modern epidemic of politicians and bureaucrats bred by journalists, it is still a more vital social act to build a house than to talk high political theories. The ploughmen and their craft are still a greater factor in life than the Cabinet Minister and his political plans. If then the organs of public opinion centre around the Minister instead of the ploughman, it is as foolish an idea as if the Entente[26] armies had concentrated on the Spanish frontier while the Germans were marshalling in Belgium: they would simply – like the newspapers – have been far away from the scene of action. It is a somewhat remarkable fact that though our modern governors and their ideas have reduced a large part of Europe and North America in particular, and the world in general, to chaos and disorder, yet they have had little more effect on humanity than if they were infants battering with their fists in the hope of pushing down St. Paul's Cathedral. They have ruined the pleasure of the world, as they have ruined so much of its beauty; the modern system has stuck a knife in the soul of the native arts, and offered us instead the servile affectations of its parasites; and yet man today still knows little but the wisdom that was taught him by his ancestors. The new things pass over his head as a cloud passes over a wheat field.

The persistent continuity of the human tradition of democratic organization, as distinguished from central government, has been brilliantly stated in a recent article on Russia.* The writer therein sums up his conclusions in the following sentence: "The society of Rome over two thousand years ago was the society of, at any rate, Great Russia only yesterday. The *mir*[27] was the Roman *gens*."[28] He quotes a remarkable prophecy by Sir Henry Maine[29] in his *Early History of Institutions:* "The soil of the older provinces of the Russian Empire has been from time immemorial almost exclusively distributed among groups of self-styled kinsmen, collected in cultivating village communities, self-organized and self-governed… and it is one of the facts with which the Western world will some day assuredly have to reckon." It is interesting that the leading law review should maintain that this great upheaval in Russia, which the confused newspaper proprietors seem to rank as a moment of temporary anarchy, is in reality based on a legal tradition which can be measured by the thousand years. To quote Mr. Strahan again: "The old Roman Commonwealth was organized politically on the basis of race, and concurrently on the basis of collective ownership; the very principles on which the Revolution has based the new Russian Commonwealth."†

That is a very recent and a very dramatic example of the main idea in this present essay. For it is an attempt to show that what we too often accept as an essential principle of human society may

---

* *The Law Quarterly Review,* January 1919, by Mr. J.A. Strahan.

† It may be necessary to add that the principles of the Russian Revolution are very probably a long, long way from the ideals of Mr. Trotsky and his Jewish friends. The thought of any Jew representing Russia can arouse nothing but bitter laughter in the historical mind.

be only a new-fangled notion when placed beside traditions which have borne the wear and tear of centuries. To prove that a thing is new is by no means to prove that it is wrong. As a matter of fact, the chief case against the modern system of centralized and political government is not that it is new, but rather that it is intolerably unsuccessful. No one can claim that the older system had no defects. It had many – the chief of these being that it was not stable enough to survive forever. But it is equally impossible to deny that the older system produced very gorgeous successes. A social organism which gave us the art and philosophy of Greece, the miraculous beauty of the stained glass of Chartres, and that subtle complexity of human endeavour which we call Florence and Padua or by the name of a hundred old cities; such is not a thing which can be lightly dismissed when it dares to assert itself against a modern society which has vomited up Liverpool and Clapham. The case must be argued on its merits, in detail; but *prima facie*, it is suggested that the judgement is not on the side of Clapham.

But there is no intention to argue here the case historically. That must be left to the historians, merely begging their readers to consider the facts, and to disregard the wonderful erection of philosophical deductions which most of our historical dons have built on their data. They are as much obsessed with the present moment and its ideals as the lightest-hearted lady at the lightest of balls. Were they only like the wise butterflies, who flit from flower to flower, the historians might realize the truth; but in truth their vision would not reach to the end of Cyrano's[30] nose. When they assume, as they almost always do, that a state is the climax of national and imperialist endeavour, one wonders if they ever read that most exciting of romances, the tale of the Roman Empire. Perhaps they did not know it was serious history, for it is, in its way, the most colossal farce that was ever written. It is the story of some imperialists (like the ones who write the *Morning Post*[31] and the butlers and ladies' maids who read them) who set out to build a great empire. They collected into their central hands more and more of the government, until Rome was first and the rest nowhere. Then the great farce began. The more power they seized, the less they had; it was like filling a can with a hole in it. There was a mighty wrestling match with the old Senate. The emperors slew the senators by the hundred, and the Senate (merely for want of emperors) replied by murdering them by the half-dozen. But the laughter grows louder and louder; when the murdering was over, neither the emperors nor the senators had won, for a vast gang of bureaucrats had quietly seized every handle of the governing state, and the Roman people were the slaves of an invisible power whom they could not even put to sword, as they had slain their emperors. So Rome perished because it became the strongest government in the world;* it was crushed by barbarians who scarcely knew what government meant. But, in truth, it was not the Teutons who ruined Rome: it was ruined by its own governors – the bureaucrats – as the British Empire will be ruined.

This introductory chapter will have served its purpose if it arouses a healthy suspicion that what is has not always been, and will not always be hereafter. It is the learned persons, who accept the present so innocently, who are parochial and short-sighted. It is the simple who seem to grasp the everlasting traditions of humanity. It is the university professors who are so often sentimentalists; it is often the peasants who know the truth. One of the hopes of the guild system is that it will replace the confused idealists, who play with shadowy fiction, and put in their place some harder-headed people who will consider the facts.

---

* By taking the Middle Ages as the most convenient type of the old system, one has been precluded from more than a passing reference to the elaborate guild system of the Roman period. The state-controlled *collegia* of the Empire should be of more than ordinary interest to those national guildsmen who do not yet see that all "national" organization tends to become bureaucratic.

CHAPTER II

The First Principle: Organization by Function

HERE IS ONE GREAT ADVANTAGE in the guild system when it comes to expounding it. It has very clear general principles; and, still better, there is one first principle which stands out by itself, beyond any possibility of misunderstanding. It may be right or wrong—but at least it is very definite and obvious. This first principle is the following: The key to social structure under the guilds is organization on the basis of function; the citizens will be organized in the groups of their trades and occupations; not primarily in their parishes or parliamentary constituencies. To a great extent, this organization has already a large place in modern societies. Thus, the shareholders of a tea plantation company may be described superficially as organized on their basis of function as tea producers. Again, the cotton operatives, organized as a trade union, may still more justly be said to be grouped by their function of producing cotton cloth. The teachers of a university are a united body because of their common function of producing learning and wisdom. The doctors are grouped by function in their Medical Association; likewise the lawyers in their Inns of Court and Incorporated Society. In short, as already suggested in the first chapter, the system of organization by function is deeply rooted in all human society.

The guild system, then, does not put forward any new principle; the distinctiveness of its theory is in the emphasis it gives to it. The guildsmen claim that organization by function or trade is by far the most vital link in the social structure, and that all other human links are very secondary beside it. Other social bonds there are, and many, but all of them are most clearly subordinate to the vastly superior importance of organization of mankind by profession and trade.

There are very few hard lines in nature; classification is not so much a fact as a convenience. Science does not state laws because they always exist, but rather because the vastness of the universe must somehow or other be made comprehensible to the limited human mind. And thus it must be realized that no classification of men can be perfectly precise. How many human beings are there who could be correctly described in terms of race? We may, for all practical purposes, quite well describe a man as English, Irish or French; but our classification would look childishly absurd if we dug to the root of his family tree. The man whom we, quite wisely, decide to call a typical Englishman, is often the product of half the races of mankind. So classification is for convenience, and we must remember that rule when we classify men by their trades.

As organization is the very basis of society, in laying down its rules we must come to some decision on the principle to be followed. Heine's[32] charming flower girl in Paris classified her blooms according to their scents, and the poet added that he had some reason to believe that she also classified men by the same rule. One can imagine an artist grouping mankind by the laws of beauty; a professor might herd them by their powers of reason; a hotelkeeper by their ability to pay for his most expensive rooms; and a politician by their capacity for accepting promises instead of fulfilment.

The guildsman, while recognizing all these classifications and the advantages thereof, maintains that there is one method of arrangement which is infinitely more useful: to wit, the classification by function. But even here one must recognize at the start that the lines must be vague to a certain degree. A postman may grow his own vegetables; a draper may keep bees; an insurance agent may keep a shop; and colonels may get trade commissions from their wine merchants. But for the normal man or woman it is fairly easy to pick out one occupation which is the chief business of life. The guild system maintains that the chief business is the central fact in the life of that citizen, and his relations with his fellow men must be largely determined by it. It is of only inferior interest to know that a citizen lives in one borough or another, in one county or another, in which he is registered as a parliamentary or local government voter. It is possible that it may even be necessary under a guild system, to keep the present political classifications by area; but the point here emphasized is the exceptional importance of the functional classifications by trade, and the comparative insignificance of all other classifications, whether by political areas or by colour of the hair. There are few absolute laws in life – it is almost entirely a matter of their emphasis.

Of all classifications of man, the most violent contrast is that between the area theory of the politicians and the functional theory of the guildsmen. They are at opposite poles. The division of citizens into geographical areas for the purpose of parliamentary representation was an idea which, looking back, one can now see growing up more or less by accident, and certainly only for a very limited purpose, as was discussed in the first chapter. A few moments' consideration of this classification by postal address will show how superficial it is. No one denies that there is a certain common bond between men because they are next-door neighbours. They are interested in the same postman and policeman; they share the same drainpipes and the same water supply. Admitted. But none of these common bonds concerns a vital principle in the man's life, on which his citizenship can be reasonably based.

At present a citizen rises (in theory) to his highest expression of citizenship when he elects the parliamentary member for his borough or county. The guildsman's case is that it is absurd that such an all-important function should be based on nothing more vital than living in the same street or the next village. Heine's flower girl had really a more intellectual case.

But it is the less necessary to argue the theoretical case for political organization by area, because its clear failure in practice alone rules it outside the schemes of intelligent beings. Politicians elected by area to do the work of the nation very obviously do not do that work. It is not done at all, or it is done very badly. If even a perfect theory works altogether imperfectly it is to all intents and purposes useless for worldly men and women. But it is strange that anyone ever imagined that this political system could work. What human being has yet appeared who could reasonably promise to represent the most varied desires and grievances of the ten or twenty thousand electors who inhabit his political area? Even if his honest desire to accomplish the work did not fail, it is all too clear that the cubic capacity of his brain was not designed for any such colossal task. Half the political adventurers in Parliament who fail to represent their constituents have really the very reasonable excuse that an archangel alone would suffice. When they set out for Westminster, they might plead that they were being sent on a wild-goose chase.

Then there is the electors' side which is equally bound for failure. How is it possible that the normal citizen could choose by the crude parliamentary system the right man for his purposes? Even assuming that such an encyclopædic creature existed, how could the voter find the man? We know, as a matter of practice, he rarely does; but the point for the moment is, how could we expect him to do so? Sometimes a parliamentary candidate is a local man; at best a mere fraction of the electors have any real knowledge of his intellect or his morals. He may promise the right programme, and he may intend to fulfil that promise. In fifty percent of the cases, both his programme and his intentions are defective, and the astounding thing is that the individual electors seem quite unable to find better candidates – such is the cumbersomeness of the parliamentary system. That is probably the main reason why the politicians have survived so long: they are entrenched behind a maze of political rules to prevent democratic attack. The elections are usually fought on issues of slight importance; or those of which the average elector has no knowledge sufficient to affect his judgement; or, again, the issues may be so complicated and conflicting that neither electors nor elected know much about them.

That is perhaps the main weakness of the parliamentary system. It deals with matters beyond its grasp, beyond the grasp of everybody except experts on the subject concerned. The parliamentary system might be all right if it could perform a first-class miracle—master the knowledge of the world and translate it into legislation. We must not be angry with Westminster for failing to perform the impossible, but we must rebuke it for even trying. A thousand subjects are put under the control of men selected by a disorganized mob of electors, with no common desires or common knowledge. The politician by appealing to everybody is able to escape being bound to anything. In the hubbub of public life he dodges the necessity for reason. The politician survives by reliance on the ignorance of his constituents.

Now there is one department of life where it is more difficult to be evasive. If a man has any exact knowledge at all, it is on the subject of his daily work. If the business placed before a meeting were to discuss the cotton trade, and legislate for it, it is more than probable that the cotton operative and the factory manager would have very definite minds of their own as to what should be done or left undone. The candidate could not escape the point by discussing the condition of the Hottentots[33] or the necessity for reforming the music hall, or a foreign policy for Timbuktu. To be tied down to cotton might lead that politician to disaster. Hence, perhaps, his frantic desire to get as many subjects as possible within the scope of Parliamentary debate.

A man's work is both his first interest and his greatest knowledge. It is by far the strongest link with his fellow men—in a material sense, that is; and matter has a very great deal to do with the spirit. If the nation were grouped into its trades rather than within its geographical areas, it would then be organized on the main principles of interest and knowledge. The trade unit would be the most compact and the best informed about its own affairs. Without for the moment discussing the theoretical side any further, it will be useful to consider how it might work out in practice if the citizens of a nation were primarily organized on the basis of their trades or occupations. Let us glance at the possibilities.

Coal mining is a comparatively simple case. It is a very definite trade; it is not seasonal or merging into other work, though it may be at first sight a little difficult to know whether the men who drive the engines of the pits are miners or engineers. But when one speaks of the coal industry the term denotes a fairly definite class. Let us assume that before the miners concerned themselves with political matters (as Westminster understands them) they were first organized as a Guild of Coal Miners. After all, what more important function of a public kind do the miners perform? Surely the digging of coal is the very essence of their work for the state. If the nation desires that coal should be dug (it is a dirty trade, but that is not the point for the moment), then who is more capable of legislating for it, and controlling the digging, than the miners? It may be suggested that the miners would only consider their own interests – the argument being based on the knowledge that the present capitalist traders, who control industry, consider little else but their personal interests. So that objection has little weight, for at the worst it would be better that the self-interests of many miners were considered than the interests of a few coal-owners.

The essence of the scheme would be that the digging of coal, as a national industry, would then be controlled by the united body of the coal miners, grouped into what may be conveniently termed a guild. That word is used instead of "company" or "association," or analogous terms, because it is desired to insist energetically on the fact that this is a group of the actual workers – whether managers or pit boys, clerks or hewers, checkers or engineers – in distinction from a "company," for instance; which is in the main a collection of shareholders, who have invested money, but whose work does not go beyond attending the annual meeting. A director who took an active part in the management would, for the purpose of this present argument, come under the head of managing staff. The exact functions of this guild, its scope and its subordination to the state will be discussed later. For the moment we are concerned in visualizing the appearance of a nation whose primary organization is on the basis of trades.

Let us turn to a very different kind of work: the profession of teaching. This is, broadly speaking, just as much a productive industry as coal mining. It is the business of miners to produce coal;

it is the function of teachers to produce educated pupils. The same arguments apply with remarkable closeness. It is a very skilled work, like the digging of coal, and the people who know most about it are the teachers and experts who devote themselves to the study of the craft—just as scientists who devote themselves to the technical processes of mining would be included in the mining guild. The grouping of educationalists into a guild (or rather into many guilds, as will be discussed later) would be as practicable a piece of public organization as the case of the miners. In such a body as Oxford and Cambridge Universities, we already have something well on the way to the guild form. The schools of each county council, both primary and secondary, might be grouped into guilds containing all the teaching staff, the heads and the assistants, perhaps down to the laboratory bottle-cleaners. As in the case of the miners, the body to whom questions of education would be primarily referred would be the Guild of Teachers.

The case of the railways is a fairly simple one, and the guild would include the whole of the directors and staff down to the humblest porter at the smallest country station. Forgetting their present method of sitting at Westminster—whether as directors and shareholders or as trade union secretaries—the railwaymen would first and foremost think of themselves as members, and therefore electors, of the Guild of Railways; and they would be primarily responsible for the management of the railroads.

Again with the doctors and lawyers. The latter are already a guild of a fairly complete kind. They have almost complete control of their profession as against the state, and internally the Bar Council is elected by the members of the profession. Those who hastily say that the guild system is absurd, must first of all explain how it is that this great absurdity has existed for so many long centuries. It is fair to confess that a small and somewhat uniform profession like the law has many advantages over such a diverse trade as engineering for example, or mining, with their innumerable grades of labour. The case of the doctors is very similar to the lawyers: they likewise have already something very near the guild form, and if they also were endowed with the guild functions, the whole matter of public health would be placed in the hands of the Medical Guilds for legislation and administration, and not be committed to the care of very inexperienced gentlemen at Westminster. The doctors would be given the task of producing good health, as the miners would have the job of producing coal.

Without going through the list of the recognized industries, it is necessary to consider how far the guild system would cover the nation as a whole. The cotton trade, iron, wool, shipbuilding, and so on, are all simple cases. But other cases are not so obvious. The retail shopkeepers might find it necessary to form a guild apart from the trade producing their goods, or they might be included in the producing guild itself. Thus the coal merchants would, under the latter alternative, be members of the Coal Mining Guild. But it cannot be said too emphatically that one of the many virtues of the guild idea is that it allows of more varieties than fixed principles. Guiding principles there are, and they are a rigid framework; but they are a constructional framework allowing of many kinds of decorations. And so it is in this case of the retail shopkeeper. It is possible that retail trade might take the form of large general stores, such as we find at present in the big towns, or the small general stores of the villages. A distributing guild would be a perfectly sensible part of a society organized by functions.

But there are the odd nooks and crannies of a state – which sometimes, perchance, are the most precious of it all. To what purpose should we become a perfectly organized industrial community if we ceased to become the home of poets and musicians and dreamers? Life as a time to be always serious and productive is nothing but a plutocratic nightmare. There are some who are only well employed when they are doing nothing – nothing at least that could be registered on a pay sheet or approved by an overseer. The tramp may be the wisest of men, just as the anarchist may have discovered more of the laws of governing than the bureaucrat. But, to put the question precisely: Will there be a Guild of Poets, and one of Musicians, and of Philosophers, and of Idle Dreamers? As for the musicians, in the sense of performers in an orchestra, it is fairly obvious that there will be, for an orchestra itself has the necessary cohesion and unity; it is itself a guild in embryo.

But a Guild of Composers is a very different matter. Composers do not do their work by gathering together in concert halls and bandstands. Schubert wrote some of his best songs by sitting in taverns, not with his fellow composers, but with very riotous persons who had a keener taste for alcohol than for scoring music. Likewise with poets; there is a, probably erroneous, tradition that they frequent moonlit shores and sunny forest glades, proceedings which it would be difficult, perhaps, to regulate by guild rules; while in the matter of output, the merits of a poem cannot be tested as one would test steel or cotton cloth. Far be it from asserting that the thing cannot be done, or that it is unwise to try. Poets, who in real life are so often the most businesslike and practical of creatures, may well be able to reduce their subtle craft to precise rules – after all, it is only a stupid bureaucrat who makes clumsy regulations which will not fit the facts. And so with stray philosophers. There are not many "philosophers" pure and simple, and they will be mainly attached to the various university staffs, as they are today. Probably the dreamer and thinker will link up with the tramps and other men of unshackled leisure, and freedom from business hours. But that is a subject which is better left in the lap of the gods.

Briefly, there is not much that is healthy in a national life which cannot be collected coherently within the guild form. For the production of wealth, from a steel steamship to a lyric, is assisted, rather than retarded, by the collective effort of the producers. It is at least arguable that the guild labour which produced the great medieval cathedrals did a greater work than was ever done by all the self-centred artists and novelists who produce secretly in their studies and studios. But, at the least, the vast bulk of the work that is necessary for a nation's health and wealth can be produced under co-operative guilds as easily as under capitalist companies. All that is left outside can be safely committed to that kindly fate which, in truth, settles so many of the affairs of human life. If the poet and artist can survive in the hideousness and callousness of the plutocrats' world, certainly he will have a better chance in a world whose essence will be the placing of happiness and beauty before banking accounts. When did the arts and crafts ever touch so high as during the age of medieval guilds?

Now the primary advantage of a system of organization by guilds will be that the arrangement of national life will be on the basis of essential work. The nation will become a machine organized for doing the nation's work. Instead of an industrial system which is not merely anarchical in the opinion of the labour agitator, but is chaotic in hard fact, we should have a society based on its natural units, like a well-classified library, a well-arranged store; where the librarians and assistants can put their hand at once on what is demanded. That is the real case for organization by function, by trade and occupation: it is a natural classification based on facts. Every normal unit of the state would be organized as a citizen in regard to his main responsibility and knowledge. He would be considered primarily as an expert, and his chief civil duty would be to do that which he really could do.

For example, it is only a farce asking the average man to give a decision concerning our relations with the South Sea Islands, when he has never seen the South Seas, their islands, or their islanders, at any closer range than a Conrad[34] romance. He may have, ultimately, to come to some decision on these matters, but it will have to be as a by-road in public life. Whereas, under the present system, a whole general election may turn on one of these mysterious political problems, and the government for the next six years may be chosen on the question whether Persia should have a parliamentary system or a benevolent despotism. So far as Englishmen are concerned, they might as well vote on a constitution for the ichthyosaurus. The guild idea is an endeavour to bring us back to reality, to base our social life on essential facts (such as the production of corn and good music), instead of asking our legislators to amuse themselves – and bore us – with the vaguest of generalities.

Under a guild system, the citizen would be asked to decide what he knew something about; a coal miner would be asked to control the mines, not the political constitution of Russia. How this would affect our relations with Russia, that is, who would constitute the Foreign Office Guild, if any, will be discussed in a later chapter. It is only maintained here, that as all social classifications must be somewhat arbitrary, we must select that which is based on the most essential factors; and, surely, the production of wealth is the chief material work of man, and his trade is the most natural and most effective organ of government. If one can fall to generalities, it may be said that the guild system in action would be the nation in battle array – every man at his post.

From the point of view of the citizens in general, the guild system would possess the advantage of allowing quick reference of any difficulty to the most expert advice. There is a threatened shortage of corn, for example. To whom could one refer the problem today? To the Board of Agriculture? It could only set in action machinery for passing on the question to the landlord, the farmer, and the peasant; in short, the Board could merely act as a middleman. It would be useless to go to the landlords, or to the farmers, or to the labourers separately and directly, because in the matter of corn production they are now merely one element in a complicated industry. Neither could speak for the others. Of course the facts could be gradually collected from these various sources; and eventually the Board of Agriculture could make a solemn report. But a report does not necessarily grow corn; the heart of the problem would still remain. Now if all the producers were already linked in a guild, the procedure would be infinitely simplified.

A guild report would be the opinion of the majority of the workers in the industry. There might be a dissenting minority; until the population of the world is reduced below three, there will probably always be a dissenting minority, and the last two will probably have to toss for a decision when they no longer can discover a chairman with a casting vote. Such is the inevitable waywardness of mankind. But so long as the majority decision is accepted, there is no better form than the guild for getting the best advice in the quickest way. There is so much more likely to be unity amongst members who all know (more or less) the facts of the case in dispute. If they differ, it will be on a matter that is really hard to decide, whereas today a parliament splits itself up into parties which are usually only fighting shadows.

Such, in bare outline, is the essential principle of the guild method of organizing the nation. In selecting the function of production – in its widest sense, which may include every form of wealth, from a coal scuttle and a match to a song or a poem – this idea goes no further than an assertion that this is the most convenient factor to select. It must not be imagined that any reasonable person thinks that this is the only possible or necessary classification. There may be a need for several systems, even running side by side. A man will be a doctor and therefore a member of his Guild of Medicine, but as a cricketer he will be a member of the cricket club; as an amateur actor, a member of the dramatic association; as a politician he may join a Society for the Abolition of the Guilds; as a philosopher he may join the Pragmatic Clique; while during his summer holiday he will appear in Switzerland under the ensign of the Alpine Club.

It is all-important to get this aspect of the matter firmly in the mind. There is no narrow dogmatism about the guild idea. It is not a despotism. It does not attempt, with the enthusiasm of a new district visitor, to clean all the dark corners of our homes and lives. In reality it attempts no more than arranging the affairs of our daily work. The one thing it does assert with some dogmatism is that, from the public point of view, there is nothing more important than this work, and that it is the most convenient basis on which we can set ourselves as a nation. There are expansive politicians, often with a mysterious craving for high finance and kindred recreations, who make great speeches about the British Empire, or those who have very gorgeous ideas concerning the Federation of the World. The guildsman is not necessarily opposed, but he cannot sometimes restrain a rather impatient turn of the shoulders: "Yes, I know, perhaps, perhaps…but just a moment, please, while we work out a system by which we can first get several rather important affairs in working order. You won't be able to voyage around your delightful Empire until the coal is dug, or until somebody builds you a ship; and you might starve even with an empire at your feet, unless somebody remembered to grow corn. Indeed, this empire of yours is really a matter for our spare hours and holiday dreams. It is almost a luxury, which can only be produced after the day's work is done."

That is the guildsman's attitude to all the other alluring dreams of social construction, to all the great adventures of the human race. He is not unsympathetic; he merely says they must come in their due order of importance. He is simple-minded enough to listen to all those village sayings about the horse coming before the cart, and the good reasons for walking before one runs. He does not profess to be very philosophical, but he does pride himself on his common sense. He thinks it is common sense to produce a well-built house before he produces an empire; he is quite ready to listen to those tales of El Dorado[35] with their promises of the wealth of the Indies to deck his house when built. But he thinks it will be safer to organize as a guild of house builders, rather than on the more illusive basis of El Dorado.

He may be short-sighted, or worse still, a coward. But the long-sighted people have disappointed us so often, while the brave men have sacrificed so many other men's lives in the pursuit of their windy ideals and bankers' paradises. So the very hard-headed guildsman has grown a little sceptical, and has suppressed his cravings for romance. He turns rather longingly to those old days when, instead of building empires and fortunes for plutocrats, men were content if they earned their own livings at their own trades. Of course it is unselfish to make fortunes for other men, and the most gigantic unselfishness was when the poor men of England built empire to enrich their masters. However, there are signs of the growth of self, and when it reaches the unselfish workers they will be more interested in their own workshops than in other people's empires. The turning of our ideals to the workshops will lead very quickly to the need for the guilds.

For the guilds will be the organization of the nation in its daily work, and the end of that loose thinking which the newspapers now call "politics."

CHAPTER III

THE SECOND PRINCIPLE: SELF-MANAGEMENT

HE LAST CHAPTER has looked at the guilds from the outside; we have merely gazed at their façades, as country cousins gaze at the dome of St. Paul's. We have, so far, no knowledge of their construction. The fundamental reason for the guild system is that it organizes the people in the order of their trades, whereby the work of the community can be done by those who best know how to do it. Therefore, it naturally follows that when once the guild is constituted, its affairs must be, in the main, controlled by the guild members; otherwise the advantage of expert management would be lost.

Nevertheless, it is possible to conceive of a guild which did its work under a fairly complete control by an external body. For example, it could be managed by a state department in Whitehall, where all the rules might be drafted, and from which the inspectors would come to see that those rules were obeyed. The guildsmen under such a system would be the servants of a superior body over which they had no control, just as they are now the servants of comparatively uncontrolled capitalists. Or the guilds, when formed, might be put under the management of a controlling trade council, whereby they would be little more than branches of a great trade combine – capitalist or democratic according to structure.

Now it must not hastily be assumed that there will not be transition guilds somewhat of this kind. Until the majority of the members of a trade will take the trouble to make themselves fully expert in its problems, it is quite clear that the guilds cannot be self-managing. A superior and beneficent autocrat might group all the people of a nation into their respective trades and occupations, and endow each group with the right to manage its own affairs. But there are very tight limits to the power of the autocrat, fortunately. He can take all his horses to the water, but he cannot make them drink – a truth which has been concealed from the babes and sucklings of the governing class, though the stable boys have known it since their first failure at the farmyard pond.

If organization by function is the first principle and the anatomical structure of the guild system, the principle of self-management is the idea which makes the dry bones of that structure move with life. So long as the guild is controlled by any outside influence, so long it is merely a babe unable to walk. As was said above, it may be as necessary a stage in its career as in the life of the child. But we are now considering this second principle in its complete form. The essence of it is that, in the main, the guildsmen are their own masters, not necessarily in any spirit of self-assertion, but just because the idea of the guild is that work shall be done by craftsmen and professionals, and not by outsiders and amateurs.

Now, of course, it is possible in theory that a central government department might engage, let us say, an experienced coal miner to advise the department on the control of the mines; to draft their regulations, to superintend their inspectors, and generally represent the state insofar as it interferes in the coal mining industry. One might even go further, and suppose that the whole central department is staffed with experienced men drawn straight from the mines or the pit heads. It will be said that here surely is a scheme which will provide the purest of expert advice. But such a system must be classed as bureaucracy; it is entirely opposed to the whole essence of the guild system – which insists on self-management, as against outside control, however expert. There are several good reasons for this insistence.

First, there is the very good reason that bureaucracy, as a matter of fact, does not choose expert workers; it chooses first-class bureaucrats. It would be inhuman if it did not look upon the world with the rather timid eyes of the sedentary clerk. It probably thinks that the world can be saved if a sufficient number of letters and reports are written about it. There are hundreds and thousands of clever, self-sacrificing officials in government offices who pass their lives in helpful work. But the most helpful work they can do is to stand on one side, and not act as a buffer between the men who are themselves producing and the community which is receiving. It is not that all government officials are dishonest or foolish; most of them are the reverse. The bad thing about them all is that they are clerks, and wealth is not made by clerks. It is standing the pyramid of production on an uneasy apex, when we attempt to balance it on bureaucracy. A pyramid, if one wishes it restful and contented, must be on its base, and the base of production is labour. There may be need for many clerks before the products reach the public; the clerk may be most necessary for many quite legitimate purposes. But he is not a base.

Bureaucracy may be willing to consult expert workers at times, but it is the exception, not the rule. Besides, why consult the producers when these latter should already have been in a position to do what is necessary without having to proceed through the tedious process of consulting anybody? Bureaucracy, at the best, must be a buffer state, and anything it does must be second-hand work. There may be a legitimate place for it; as we shall see later, there must be some kind of social organ representing the community, something we call the "state," and there it will be difficult to dodge the sedentary clerk and his assistant officeboy altogether. But wherever we eventually place him, it will not be as a base. As one has already insisted in another connection, the guild system is not dogmatic; it is largely a question of arranging our social affairs with the right emphasis, of getting that nice balance which is so often the real answer to the wordy squabbles of this world. So often we are all nearly right, it is only a matter of saying what we mean in the correct tone.

Perhaps the most urgent practical reason for self-management by the guild members is that it is becoming clearer than clarity that, for good or evil, democracy has arrived. The current phrase is that it is knocking at the door; it almost looks as though it has knocked the door down. There is a healthy reaction against doing what we are told. In many cases it may be admitted that what we are told is wiser than what we do ourselves. But doing the wrong thing ourselves is often more stimulating than doing the right thing because somebody else orders it. The boys who are tied to their mother's apron strings are proverbially a poor lot. And whether the apron belongs to a bishop, a state official, or a private master, a long course of leading tends to intellectual flabbiness. When democracy insists that it should do its own work and revolts against its masters, it is a principle that can be defended by the rules of the science books. And, right or wrong, democracy is wilful and clearly intends to try.

But the soundest reason for self-management in a guild is that it is clearly impossible to find a better way of doing the work. Who knows more about the digging of coal than the coal miners and their foremen and managers? Can the wisest men at the Board of Trade know anything that the miners do not know first? Who knows more about the spinning of cotton than the cotton spinners? It is inconceivable that any state department sitting at Whitehall should know as much about an industry as they know in the workshops or mines. Who knows as much about medicine as the doctors? Or of painting as the painters? Self-management by the trade seems almost to rank with the axiom of Euclid on self-evident propositions. To deny them is not so much argument as dull stupidity. The capitalists may have a case against guild management, but the state certainly has none whatever—at the least, it has scarcely a sporting chance.

If the master has a plausible case for managing his factory without interference by the workers, it is overridden by the fact that the workers have made up their minds differently. That is a fact which has to be recognized by wise people. If a man had two more feet where his arms are, it would be wise and scientific to tell him to walk after the manner of the other four-footed creatures. When he has evolved a pair of hands instead of two more feet, then the phenomenon must be accepted as a factor in his problem. Intellectually or morally, he insists on standing on his hind feet and nature has accepted the position, and sealed the bargain by turning the top pair into hands. And that is exactly the position of the labouring classes today. The man who tries to oppose this demand is not a brave statesman; he is a blind fool. He is trying to solve his problems by leaving out half the factors. One would not start planning a journey to America by assuming that the ocean was dry, and that the journey could be done in a car.

Consider in a little detail how the self-management theory would work out in practice, and leave the fine elaboration of theory to those very numerous persons of bureaucratic mind who love much theorizing. The general comment may be made in this place that the very essence of the guild theory is that the arrangements of management shall be made by each guild for itself. It is therefore absurd and paradoxical to draw up elaborate rules and constitutions for the various trades. That could only be done by someone who is a real bureaucrat at heart, and not a believer in the guilds at all. One can go no further than guesses at the rules the members will probably lay down to meet the special facts of the special crafts. Wise men will hope, above all else, that there will be no uniformity in the details; for that will probably mean that the problems have been solved in the crudely generalized manner which is more usually the result of the present clumsy system of central control, whether by Whitehall or by trusts. The guilds are advocated in the hope that they will be delicate and not clumsy in their handling of the problem of industry – and delicacy will demand special rules to meet special cases. It will be analogous to the difference between producing by hand and manufacturing by standardized machines. The guild system is government by craftsmen; the centralized monarchy or plutocracy is government by machine.

The two faces to the problem are: on one side the guild producing the goods; on the other, the general public demanding and consuming those goods. In essence there is just the same problem today: the manufacturer producing and the public buying. The problem is to what extent, if any, should the public interfere with the management of the production. When the shopper goes to the bootmaker he does not first inquire into the management of the boot factory; if the goods required are in the shop, they are bought; if not, another shop is visited. Such is the present method. It must not be too hastily assumed that the consumers will any more interfere with the producers under a reformed system.

It will here be objected that under the present system there is already an elaborate control of the factory by legislation of an embracing kind, regulating the hours, the wages, the health of the workers, and so on. To that extent it is true to say that the purchaser has already interfered with the producer through his representatives at Westminster and Whitehall, and under the guild system an analogous control will be exercised. However free a hand the community as a whole will give to the guilds in self-management, there will be a standard of life on which the state will insist as a minimum. It will be rather as if the Creator gave the scientists a free hand with their own special departments, so long as they kept regard to the great universal principles of gravitation and the dispersal of energy. The geologist could sort out his epochs and strata to his fancy; the biologist arrange and rearrange his species; the sociologist lay down his laws for human civilization. They would each have self-management up to a point.

In a similar way the state will lay down general principles which even self-managing guilds must respect. There will be probably a minimum wage based on a theory that below it no citizen could keep himself in the condition which the public honour and welfare demand. Beyond that minimum one imagines that each guild will be allowed to distribute its surplus as the members decide by a vote of the majority. It is very improbable that they will vote at first for equality of wages. To begin with, there will be a fairly united refusal of the full-aged and experienced members to accept equality with the young apprentices. Even the most rabid disciple of Liberty, Equality, and Fraternity will not necessarily demand the same wage for a youth of eighteen learning his trade and a full-trained man of thirty-five, and once the principle was broken, Equality would become a mere rough-and-ready standard against which to measure each case as it arose, in order to strike a balance within reasonable limits. This guild, for its own welfare, would almost certainly offer higher wages to anyone whose special encouragement to work would be for the advantage of the whole. For example, if one member had given proof of high organizing powers, it would obviously be to the advantage of the members to incite him to apply that power to the highest possible degree. It would save them time and money, and therefore increase their profits. For, as will be discussed later, there is no reason to think that the guilds will immediately abolish competition. It will be made a sane competition for the benefit of the community, instead of a very insane one, for the benefit of the profiteer. But it would be just as hasty to assume that all competition is a public evil as it would be for a man with sunstroke to dismiss the sun as a public nuisance. Anyhow, if competition between guilds remains, it will be to the advantage of the members to pay enticing rewards for the most experienced managers and officials. All of which distinctions of reward will be for the members to decide within the standard laid down by the state in its first principles.

Then there may well be a state standard of hours of work. Here again it can be nothing beyond a maximum which must not be passed, on the general grounds that the health and happiness of the citizen may be injured to the detriment of the honour and welfare of the community. And likewise there may be standardized laws of health and general safety. But with democratic guild control the urgent necessity for this national minimum legislation will somewhat disappear. It is necessary under a control by profiteers and company promoters – but quite another thing when the workers make their own regulations for their own welfare.

At what point state general principles will cease, and the equally great state principle of self-management begin, cannot be decided by any hard-and-fast boundary lines. It will not be a straight line, like the artificial lines of many modern American states. It will turn back and forward to suit the convenience of those innumerable bends and fancies of the human mind. Only dull-witted persons demand inelastic rules; wise people will be content with a mere outline which can be modified as circumstances arise.

Of course the general rule will be that all technical points concerning the processes of production will be entirely under the control of the guild. Put in another way, it will be for the state to express *what* it wants; it will be for the guild to say *how* it shall be done. Within the general standard of public morality and culture, as laid down by the collective desire of the community and expressed by its organ the state, the guild will be given a free hand. As already hinted, this freedom will not necessarily be given because one governing class suddenly becomes generous and unselfish, but mainly because it is becoming every day more impossible for reasonable men to deny the soundness of the argument that the only people who can properly control production are the people who produce. That is the chief strength of the guild idea – it is based on quite ordinary common sense, divorced from that sentimentality which is the real basis of most plutocratic and bureaucratic government. The state will not interfere with the guilds more than it can help, for exactly the same reason that a mother does not interfere with the surgeon whom she has called to operate on her child. One leaves a job to the man who can do it best.

There will naturally be great variety in the form of the guilds, and consequently, a great variety in the methods of management. If the guild system is to cover everything from dairy farming to university education, and all work from the production of plates to the playing of musical symphonies, then it is fairly clear that there may be more differences than similarities in their internal rules. The breaking up of a trade into smaller local units, instead of having one vast guild covering the whole industry, is so important an internal need that it will be discussed by itself as an independent first principle in the next chapter. But the present is the most convenient place to consider other internal problems of management which may affect the guild.

Having received a charter from the state (which will be discussed in a later chapter), it will be the legitimate right of the guild to take as much advantage and profit from that charter as an honest private trader takes from a contract with a customer. The guilds will take the place of the private master or public company, and the problems of management which they will inherit from their predecessors will often equally apply to their own case. As already suggested, the members will have selfish reasons, if nothing better, for selecting the most efficient staff of officials and managers. The capable manager, who is now probably afraid that a revolution in the industrial system may dislodge him from his place, might realize that the most revolutionary of guilds would think twice before they lost the services of an efficient official. They will then be as anxious to secure efficient managers as the capitalists are anxious to find and keep them today, and this for the same reason – the increased prosperity of the business. In some cases, the guilds may decide to make all appointments of officers in a full meeting, by popular vote. But others may be quite willing to leave selections and promotion to the managerial staff, leaving criticism for the annual meetings, and opportunities when a contract with an offending manager might be closed. It is quite possible that for the sake of good managers a guild may give lengthy contracts to its officials; but it will probably not bind itself over too many meetings without a very excellent reason. But here, as elsewhere, there will be infinite variety in the rules.

Another way of considering the position of officers is to realize their changed status in a guild where they will be much more clearly overseers of work than of workmen. In other words, the foremen and managers of today are so largely needed to keep the workers at full pressure, and only in part are they necessary for superintending the work as a process. But when a worker is just as much interested in his business as the capitalist is now, every man will be a jog on the fellow who is inclined to laze; while on the other side there will be fewer inclined to be slack than there are today, when the main result of hard work is to make somebody else richer than he has the right to be. So the main gist of the foreman and overseer under the guilds will be to assist in increasing the efficiency of the process. The workers, so far as they keep the election of officials in their own hands, will be mainly guided in their choice by their knowledge of a candidate's technical skill.

It is difficult to exaggerate the technical advantages of giving every worker, humanly and legitimately, a selfish interest in the welfare of his guild. It should easily reduce the managing staff by a large fraction, for there will be less slacking and everybody will be interested in doing his best. To substitute the element of collective welfare for the private capitalist's welfare will cause most radical changes in industry; it is, indeed, almost impossible to measure them, or even to know of what precise nature they will be. Until they are known and measured more exactly, it is perhaps a waste of time discussing in too great detail the structure of the guilds of the future. It is the main idea of the present essay to define clearly the general principles of the guilds – one of which is that the details must be left to the more or less individual taste and judgement of the guildsmen.

It is sufficiently obvious that it will be far more in general principles than in details that an agricultural guild will resemble a housebuilding guild. The geographical area will be quite different; the number of the members; the needs of management. Under such circumstances, the main principles will be bound to need different methods; otherwise the principles themselves might disappear. A rule that saved the principle in one case might ruin it in another. When the idea of the guilds as a whole is grasped, the details will follow as the members – and perhaps the less reasonable fates! – will care to make them. It must never be forgotten that deep down in the guild idea is the conviction that there is something inherently vicious in all compulsory government, and that self-control is the key to many of the problems of human society. It may ultimately come to pass that the governors and wise men of a state will not rule the people – as policemen and generals understand that subtle term "rule" – but will, rather, suggest to them what they ought to do. Of course the people may not always be wise enough to take the advice, and may suffer accordingly. But at least they will not suffer so much as they have continually done by obeying the commands of the third-rate intellects – and first-class adventurers – who often rule them today.

CHAPTER IV

THE THIRD PRINCIPLE:
DECENTRALIZATION AND
SMALL UNITS

AVING SEEN that the main principle of the guild system is the organization of the nation in terms of industrial function and that it naturally follows that the units so formed should have the power of self-management, if we are not going to rob the scheme of one of its greatest advantages, we now have to consider the other main and third principle which will develop the guild system as far as main principles can carry it. The rest will be practical details. The third main principle may be defined thus: No guild should be larger than the smallest possible unit that the efficiency of the trade or occupation demands. Here is a principle which is the exact contrary of almost every "orthodox" theory in history or economics for the last hundred and fifty years. The books written by the "donish" mind of the university schools, almost always start with the assumption that civilization, as expressed both in political constitutions and commercial and industrial affairs, has been a continually advantageous increase in the centralization of the governing factor. For example, the average historian assumes that France became a happier and a better governed land in proportion as the central power in Paris crushed out of existence the more local authorities of the provincial barons and communes. Again, on the economic side, it is assumed by the learned professors who have such an enthusiastic admiration for the industrial revolution (which turned so much of England into a pigsty and a coal hole) that trade got more healthy and efficient in proportion as it crushed out the small producer, and collected what was left of

him into centralized factories which, in continuation of the same beneficent process, then became pawns under the control of still more gigantic trusts.

In discussing this subject of the supposed advantages of centralization we are approaching one of the great delusions of the human race, or rather of that, fortunately small, section of it which has smothered its experience of real life in a maze of fancies. The learned have taught that centralization has been a great fact of history, and in so doing they are very obviously right; it is a fact. But to call it an event which has been beneficial to humanity is not a fact—but merely a wild guess which is disproved by the evidence. Ever since the Middle Ages, there has been a tendency for all political and economic organization to grow more and more centralized. The Middle Ages themselves were a reaction against the colossal centralization of the Roman Empire. But, of course, there will be no attempt here to treat of the subject in the way of history. For the proof of the above statement would be the history of the human race, at least in Western Europe. On one side it would be the story of this gradual tendency to centralization, both of the political organism and of the economic organs. On the other side, looking at it from the point of impartial criticism, the philosophical historian would be compelled to the conclusion that this centralization of government has been nothing short of a calamity to mankind.

Centralization has meant, in practice, the triumph of the governor over the governed. The process has been artfully, sometimes, indeed, artlessly and innocently, concealed under a maze of words which suggest that it has meant the triumph of the people as a nation or as a race. It has often, indeed generally, gone side by side with that superficial and very illusory display of "democracy" called the extension of the franchise. Because all France (more or less, and without the women) can now put in the ballot boxes its views on the government that it desires, there is a hysterical idea that Frenchmen have now more control over their affairs than they had in the days of Hugh Capet.[36] If all government is gathered together in the hands of a little group of Ministers, the people nurse the delusion that it is themselves who have elected that group. Perhaps it would be fairer to say that the people as a whole are not quite so dull and short-sighted; but it is perfectly fair to say that the orthodox philosophers and historians and economists, who translate facts into theories, have done everything in their power to foster this gigantic error in the public mind. Gigantic error, it certainly is. It is a loose reading of the superficial facts, imagining that they are the governing factors. Whereas they are such trivial facts that they would scarcely be noticed by the judicial observer.

The growth of despotism and the decline of democracy may be measured very accurately by the cubic capacity of the government offices. This may seem a paradoxical statement, but it is really a clear truth. What is more, it rests on a very simple foundation which requires no vague philosophical explanation. The key can be put very simply. It is hard to control an official or a council of men whom one rarely or never sees; it is impossible to see through brick walls and wooden doors, especially when they are many miles away. That may sound a commonplace reason for the secret strength of a central government, and yet there is really no need to search for a more ponderous one. The fundamental reason for the immunity of a central government from popular control is mainly that it is out of range of the people's guns, to put it in a simple military analogy.

If the councillors of a modest little country town ventured to do a quarter of the autocratic things done by the Westminster politicians, their burgesses would simply call at the various shops or villas possessed by the aforesaid councillors and argue with them over the counter – or if necessary with bricks through the windows. A healthy people, in full possession of their tongues – not to mention their arms – would not put up with much nonsense from their rulers if these latter lived and officiated within a reasonable distance for an evening or afternoon call. It is distance – and very little else – that tells so heavily in favour of the central government. The man who lives next door could not be a tyrant on any dangerous scale, for the simple reason that one could do so many annoying things in retaliation. A well-instructed dog barking at night could drive the most perverse of tyrants into capitulation within a week. No one dreads the known or is deceived by him—especially when he lives next door.

But who can reach Whitehall? And when one arrived, for whom would the reforming democrat ask? Centralized government, which has collected so much of the public work into one spot, has thereby succeeded in concealing the culprit from the victim of his inefficient rule. There are tens of thousands of officials in a great government. Who is the one responsible? Behind which of those thousands of windows and doors does he sit? Through how many of those corridors and rooms will a letter wander if one writes to tell him of his sins; and since he is so safely out of reach, will he much worry if your letter does reach him?

Besides, there is another side to the pernicious system of centralization. It is so vast and complex that the most honest of officials or Members of Parliament do not know how to put right that which is wrong. It resembles the maze: it is exceedingly hard to find the way. But this maze of overcentralized government is so unutterably confusing, even to the fairly expert, that it confounds itself. It would be a failure, even if every bureaucracy and every politician were as honest as the sunlight. But then, even sunlight dazzles and blinds. The system attempts too much. When the Norman and Plantagenet kings first deliberately attempted centralized government in England, it is probable that it did simplify the problem of law and order. Of course, they were under no illusions why they wanted the new method of the King's Courts instead of the older local controls of the Anglo-Saxons: it was in order to strengthen their own power. There was no humbug about the welfare of the people in those franker days. However, up to a point, there were good enough reasons for their action. But the hopelessly overcentralized government of today has outstripped all reasons, and become an ever-increasing advantage to the corrupt and inefficient, and an ever-decreasing good to the honest and efficient. The proofs are to be found in all modern history.

But it may be asked how all this touches the matter of the guilds. Very closely indeed. It was probably as a reaction against the evils of overcentralization that the more far-seeing began to turn to the older system which existed before the central theory was pushed to the point of stupidity. If organization by function is the root of the guild system, the necessity to escape the preposterous evils of centralization is certainly its driving force. But there are still too many people, within the fold, as it were, who have only half digested the theory of guilds; who have even now failed to see that it might be possible to so centralize the guilds that they would be in reality only the old state Collectivism with nothing new about it except a new name. Take the case of coal mining. It is such a vast industry that, even as a guild, it would be quite worthy of a department in Whitehall, all to itself, with a politician and Minister to represent it in the Houses of Parliament. In other words, all the evils from which the guildsmen are endeavouring to escape, would be established once more. The pits might be managed by miners, but their headquarters staff at Whitehall, or wherever they housed it, would soon be drawn from the men who lived by their pens and reports, instead of by their picks. Once more the wire-pullers and intriguers would find that peculiar element of centralization – neither land, air, nor water – which is so fertile for the propagation of the self-seeking. Soon the mines would be controlled by the bureaucrats instead of the miners – for, under the central system, Whitehall or its like will always win.

Even if the miners at the pits retained their right to vote in the election of all officials, one could see the day soon coming when they would be asked to support a candidate whom they had never seen. He would be, perchance, one of the pets of Whitehall who please those mysterious gentlemen who sit in the high seats of the ruling set. The miners might have begun to see his name appearing more and more frequently as the signature after the many byelaws and regulations with which a confident bureaucracy would soon flood the mining world. Unless a bureaucracy produces many rules, people might begin to think that it was scarcely worth its wages; so in self-defence, it naturally makes as many regulations as it can, for the same natural reason that the miners produce as many tons of coal as possible. One at least will give the bureaucrat his due; he likes to produce as many rules as he can for his salary. The root of the evil is that it is practically impossible to make a proper choice at an election – whether it be for Parliament, a local council, or for guild officials – unless the electors have a really intimate knowledge of the candidate. For this reason, it is necessary to select a unit of election which will make it reasonably possible to be offered a known candidate, instead of the professional carpetbagger, who desires to know his constituency during an election, and to see as little of it as possible before or afterwards. The large, nonfunctional basis of the present parliamentary constituencies gives every facility for the unknown carpetbagger. Men in the mass are both honest and reasonable. But the centralized system of government gives the dishonest and stupid their chance. And few will deny that they have seized it.

No sane electorate would choose an intriguer and self-seeker if he were recognized to be such, but he can hide himself behind the complicated maze of the governing system, which hides his vices – while it equally conceals the virtues of the efficient and honest.

Take in some detail the position of a guild electing its governing body, comparing a highly centralized guild with a smaller local one. There will be, or should be, two main factors influencing the elections in both cases. The members of the guild should have two points clearly in their mind: first to pick a man skilled in the technical processes of the craft, that is, an efficient workman or manager; secondly to choose the candidate who combines this industrial skill with the moral honesty which will lead him to use it for the collective good of the whole guild. In other words, the two primary characteristics of a candidate for office must be knowledge and honesty. He is an optimist indeed who imagines that such are the qualities that emerge out of the turmoil of a parliamentary general election today.

A guild member will have an infinitely better chance of firsthand knowledge of a candidate's skill than can happen in the present parliamentary case. To begin with, the chief question at issue will be the technical problems of his own trade, not those vague generalities

72

which politicians prefer to discuss at election time. Generalities are the refuge of the ignorant. When the guild candidate asks for votes, he will have to make out his case before a constituency which really knows what he is talking about. It will not be possible to ride off on the wings of eloquence, with the liberty of the Negroes of Central Africa, or the glories of the British Empire, as one's inspiring theme. The question at issue will be: How do you intend to manage this factory, or this mine, or that farm? Then eloquence will have to stand on one side for some more practical details, which may be very hampering to the eloquent. The electors will probably ask for those disagreeable things called "facts."

Besides, there is another factor in a guild election. In the natural course, a candidate will be a member of the guild – though it is conceivable that he might be enticed out of another guild by the offer of a better position – which would be a perfectly healthy competition, surely. But in the majority of cases, the candidate would be known not merely by his election address (which is often his first appearance before the electors today) but still more profoundly by his daily work in their own factory or building yard. Try to realize the position of a candidate when his daily record was in the minds of his constituents. It would not be much good giving a glowing account of one's marvellous capacity, if every man in the room had tested that capacity for himself a dozen times a week for months or years. It would be unnecessary to explain one's wholehearted unselfishness in the service of the guild, when the audience would have far better grounds for passing judgement than most juries who have to decide between guilt and innocence. Election in a guild would turn on matters of fact, and very little on matters of theory. It would depend far more on the performances of the past and very much less on promises for the future.

But the possibility of dealing with facts rather than generalities, and the consequent chance of selecting competent and honest candidates instead of incompetent adventurers; all this will vanish to a large degree if the guilds become so large that the intimate knowledge between electors and elected cannot exist. Suppose there is only one Coal Mining Guild, including all the coalfields of the country in one body. Of course, it would be possible for each district, or each pit, to elect its local and minor official. But, sooner or later, if the controlling council is to represent the whole of the British pits, a guildsman in the Scottish districts may have to decide on the merits of a proposed managing-staff man who comes from South Wales, whom he has never seen in his life. This candidate will be to all intents nothing but the old carpetbagger all over again.

Besides, it is difficult to see any easy way of working between local senior officials appointed by the National Guild and the minor local officials chosen by the pit. There is here an almost inevitable source of friction. That is no complete answer to the national system, one willingly admits, for there is inevitable friction inherent in all social organizations, and it would be childish to expect to find any system which would be free from it; this would be expecting the impossible. All one can reasonably ask is that a system with less possibility of friction should always be chosen, other things being equal, than one causing more. It is all a matter of degree.

This question between national and local guilds seems to go to the very root of the matter, and is no mere detail. Self-management under the national system would be little more than a name; it would be scarcely more control by the members of the guild than if they were all units of a state department under bureaucrats in Whitehall, which is what in essence they would be. It is not a matter of theory, but of hard fact. The question is: Could the members have any real hand in their own management if the candidates were the choice of all Britain? In theory, one knows perfectly well that we are all supposed to have a controlling hand in the British Empire under the parliamentary system. In practice, no one is so stupid as to imagine any such nonsense. Our political life is made up of these delusions; and if we are going to transfer them to a new guild system, then we might spare ourselves the pangs of the new creation. The people who talk in terms of great national guilds have usually missed the whole essence of the creed.

There is a rough-and-ready test of the electoral system: Can the elector have any really intimate knowledge of the capacity and character of the candidate he is selecting? If he cannot have this knowledge, then there is little good in worrying about the exact method of election; the issue could quite as well be decided by the returning officers tossing a penny until the election was decided on the heads-and-tails system. There must be either real knowledge, or the whole matter is a sheer farce. If anyone can discover a way of combining this intimate knowledge with a large area of election, then it would appear that squaring the circle, the alchemist's stone, the elixir of life, and other engrossing pursuits of the absolute, are all outdone. If we once decide that democracy is the necessary keynote of modern civilization, then the small electoral and functional area seems indispensable. Without it we can have benevolent despotism, partially efficient bureaucracy, blatant plutocracy, or well-meaning aristocracy. But democracy will remain nothing more living than a dream, pleasant or unpleasant as our taste may deem it. We may decide that we do not find democracy an inevitable necessity; but once choosing it, we must find the small area or utterly fail.

As suggested above, one practical difficulty would be in controlling locally elected minor officials by centrally elected seniors. Of course, it exists today in various forms. The officials of a local education board are in fact controlled by the inspectors of the Board of Education. But the theory in that case is that the local authority is independent; but if it obeys the instructions of the central Board, it receives an annual grant, and loses it if the instructions are disobeyed. So that in such a case the acceptance of the central control is an act of voluntary submission. It is perhaps here that the solution of the difficulty will be discovered.

There may conceivably be a system of independent local guilds, each entirely responsible for its own decisions and acts, and each an independent unit in its relation with the state. But it is clearly possible to offer inducements whereby the local guilds for their own advantage, if for nothing else, will be linked with the other guilds of the industry, forming a more or less coherent body or assembly, which would express the united will of the trade. A concrete example will be more descriptive than theory.

Take the building trade. It covers the whole country in its operations, and its methods and problems must be very different in different parts. A guild building country cottages and farms will need many broad and subtle distinctions which would make it uncomfortable under the control of men mainly engaged in building factories and streets of houses in towns. And quite apart from that distinction, the stonemason guilds of the north may have different views from the bricklaying guilds of the south; and even if they had the same views, they are separated by a few hundred miles. But in spite of their differences, they have the common quality that they are all builders. It will be all important for their own welfare that they should very frequently meet for the interchange of opinions concerning all that they possess in unity.

Common sense, without coercion from the state, would surely quickly bring about the formation of a National Building Congress where all the local building guilds could be represented, where they could give good advice and receive it in return from their fellow craftsmen of the building trade. But note the essential difference between this National Congress and the suggestion of a National Builders' Guild. In the case of the latter, the National Guild, the central body, once elected, would be a coercive body. A resolution passed by it, a law sanctioned by it, would be binding on all members of the guild, and would control the local units. Whereas in the case of the Congress, the association would be voluntary; the united resolutions would be nothing more than advice, which the local guilds might follow or reject at their goodwill.

This difference between government by coercion and government by voluntary agreement has not yet been fully worked out by the sociologist. It may well be that a decision as to their respective legitimate fields might clear up a great many of the problems of government. The voluntary system is very intimately connected with the guild system, which will lose its whole essence if there be any attempt to crush it into the coercive mould of the old centralized political system. In practice, it certainly seems very possible to solve the differences between the local and national guild ideals on these lines, thus getting the best of both worlds.

The local guild would send delegates certainly for annual, per-haps even for quarterly or monthly, congresses which would consider the common problems of their trade. The advice of the majority would be expressed in the ordinary way by a vote, and as advice it would be conveyed to the local bodies. In certain cases, it is conceivable that the guilds would send their delegates with power to make a binding contract with the rest. It might be a promise to maintain a fixed price, or fixed hours, or fixed wages. There would naturally be no reason to forbid a guild making contracts with its fellow guilds, so long as it did not break its fundamental charter with the state. Thus the National Congress or Association might become coercive if the members deliberately choose to bind themselves. But fundamentally, it would be a voluntary and advisory body, unless it were otherwise decided. The coercion would be in each individual case a matter of expediency, and not already decided as a matter of general theory.

There is little doubt that, in almost every case, the guilds would quickly decide that it was to their advantage to keep a permanent staff of officials as a nucleus for their periodical congresses. It would be the duty of these permanent officers to act as the intelligence department or clearing-house for the whole trade. The figures of supply and demand, the price of materials, in short everything that the intelligent private trader tries (usually without perfect success) to discover today, would be placed before the guilds by their expert clerks and statisticians. Here would be kept the records of the trade, the library of technical books, perhaps the laboratories for industrial research. Indeed, there is no reason to limit the scope of such a central organ, nor is there any reason to dread its illegitimate power, so long as it kept firmly to its ideal of voluntary action; unless, after the maturest deliberation, it decided otherwise in any particular case.

Here would seem to be the right blending of the local with the central: the most generous freedom of independence to the local guild—for the practical reason that only freedom is healthy or even possible, in the long run (for the healthy man demands it)—with the most complete unity for advice and co-operation and education that the goodwill of the collected guilds can devise. It is only the despot and the bureaucrat who are unable to conceive of unity without coercion.

THE ENTRANCE TO THE TAILORS' HALL

BACK LANE, DUBLIN

CONSEQUENT RESULTS OF
MAIN PRINCIPLES

N THE THREE PREVIOUS CHAPTERS have been defined the three main principles on which the guild system stands. In practice they would admit of many very various developments, none of which would be necessarily an essential part of the idea; they might or might not follow, according to the particular local or industrial circumstances of each case. Indeed, the guilds will probably develop in some such varied way. But without the three principles already discussed in this book, there would be no guild idea at all; they are the minimum without which it would be another system altogether, or no system at all. To repeat these three dogmas in brief. First: the main basis of the organization of public life should be a classification by function or trade, because it is the most important fact in a citizen's public career. A man's work is his most important contribution to his state, and his citizenship mainly revolves round it. Secondly: the guilds must be self-managed, for the reason that the workers of a trade are the people who best know its processes and can develop it on the most productive lines. It is in this way that the material object of the guild system (i.e., the production of wealth) can be most successfully encouraged. Thirdly: if the guilds do not avoid the highly centralizing tendency of modern society, then they will become bureaucratic, with all its endless evils.

But, having been dogmatic to that extent, it is only possible to discuss the consequences of these principles rather as suggestions. For there is a liberality of thought in this system of the guilds which is innate in it—though not innate in all its disciples.

So many disciples have betrayed their masters. If we really mean that the workers (in the fullest sense of hands and head) should be organized in many quite small guilds with comparative independence in each, then it naturally follows that we must intend to accept the very varied decisions that will inevitably follow. If we desire a rigid dogma and only one, then naturally we shall turn to bureaucracy and the machine-made mind.

A. Variety of Experiments

It is when one realizes the varied possibility of guild decisions that one can grasp perhaps the first of the secondary principles to be discussed in this chapter. A serious charge against collectivism was that it tended to a dull uniformity. For the moment it might be the right uniformity, and if there were any hope of having found the final form of social organization, then one might have been satisfied. But even if it is right today, surely it is at once necessary to start doubting whether it will be right for the new circumstances of tomorrow, when today's system may easily be wrong. Now in the variety of guild experience it may well happen that we shall find just what we want. There will be that interplay of forces and ideas which will have progress as their natural result, rather than consciously seek it. Freedom of movement is one of the essentials of a healthy life either in body or mind. Tradition is the knowledge that comes from many experiences – and it is almost the only knowledge that it is safe to trust.

B. Sane Competition

From this follows another important possible result. The guilds will save all that is good in competition which capitalism and collectivism would certainly have threatened. Driven desperate by the unutterable results of competition in practice, there were many brave people amongst us who tried to prove (and believe) that it was altogether evil and that we could do without it. As a theory for latter-day saints, there was a great deal of truth in our brave arguments. As a practice for present-day sinners, we were trying to bury our heads in the sand. The gentle prick of competition develops an energy in man, although the thing that the plutocrats call competition today is a crude affair that arouses no energy, but merely bludgeons its victims to death. There is a vital distinction between playing the piano and dancing on it.

Competition under the guild system would not necessarily be the scramble it is today. It is probable that certain limits would be defined by the terms of the guild charters granted by the state, and there would be no possibility of driving an opponent out of the market by sweating. All those crude methods would be ruled out by the reality of self-management – for workers would scarcely consent to sweat themselves. It would not be a crude competition between individual traders, which is necessarily very wasteful, because the factors are so vague that it is difficult to measure them; hence, for example, prices may be cut below what is necessary. The competition between guilds would be restricted to a very limited field. There would be only a certain number of guilds authorized to trade within a definite area, for that would be quite a legitimate curb on the competitive instinct. No guild would be encouraged to roam the land to make its fortune, as it were. The elements of competition would therefore be definitely known, and beyond concealment. The resulting frankness would remove one very disagreeable element in existing trade rivalry, its intriguing nature. Competition between the guilds would rather take the form of a semi-public contest – somewhat like the open competition of architects for a public building – though the judges would not be town councillors wire-pulling jobs for their friends!

If the human passion for strife can be preserved, yet tamed almost, with due curbs on its vulgarities, surely that will be an advantage. At the very least, it should meet the case of those stubborn people who said they themselves were quite unselfish enough to accept socialism, only they saw in it the ruin of man by making him too like a peaceful sheep. If we can prove this point, so many of our opponents will be brought face to face with their unselfishness.

Surely there will be many advantages if just a healthy competition – and not more than healthy, remember – can be maintained in a town between, for example, a reasonable number of competing bakers' guilds. It would not be a matter of six bakers' carts from different shops calling on six next-door neighbours, which must frequently happen today. That is not healthy competition, but competition run raving mad. But it would be another matter if we had the choice between two or even three breadmaking guilds within our ward. There would probably be a definite area of trade laid down in their charter, for the community would have the right to prevent the waste of transit if an avaricious guild tried to gather its trade at a recklessly extravagant cost of delivery. There are other trades where the advantages of competition could never be worth its disadvantages. For example, nobody would think it good policy, as a normal thing, to build more than one railway line between the same places. There is not that delicate personal touch in running a railway that there is in handling dough, and further, a railway line is always a nasty scar across a countryside

C. Peaceful Transition

There is another very valuable advantage in the guild system over any other suggestion for social reform. Only the illiterate still believe in the Revolution as a mode of social advance. The one thing inevitable about a revolution is its destructiveness. Force is almost always immoral, because it means the supremacy of crude muscle over more subtle brains. There are, of course, moments in history when the ultimate human right of personal dignity gives the corresponding right of self-defence, and self-defence may sometimes, on the surface, take an aggressive form. But as a normal fact in history, revolutionary and physical force is always useless, just because it does not do what it professes to do. It does not reform anything, but rather destroys most things.

Even the more apparently peaceful industrial revolutions, when blood is not shed, are equally destructive in the end. Try to estimate the colossal loss of human energy and life caused by the sudden change in the factory system which began in the eighteenth century. People were not shot in the streets, perhaps, but they were starved and stunted at home, which came to a worse thing in the long run. Indeed, the Industrial Revolution probably wasted more human life and energy than all the wars of the last two centuries together.

It seems to be an inevitable quality of human nature that it cannot undergo sudden changes. A system which demands any sudden changes is ruled out of court, not necessarily because it is illogical in itself, but simply because man is not capable of violent breaks in his traditions. One might as well assume that he could tomorrow morning have breakfast while standing on his head. Revolution assumes the impossible.

Now the guild system does seem to have those malleable qualities which allow of gentle changes. It assumes nothing sudden; it agrees that man will be tomorrow not so very different from what he is today. He may wear different clothes; he may ride in a taxi instead of a two-horse bus or a sedan chair. But at heart, he will be not very unlike the men and women whom William the Conqueror found here more than eight hundred years ago. Reformers do not always realize that it is the deep-rooted qualities of human nature that make or mar their schemes. They think that if they can modify some surface fact, if they can make men live in a cottage instead of camping on a common, that they have made some radical difference. Nothing could be further from the truth. The chief failing of reformers is that they know so little about men. Their operations on the human organism are wonderfully reminiscent of what would happen if an earthly surgeon began to operate on a man from Mars, of whose internal machinery he knew nothing.

But the guild system makes no sudden demands. It holds out no sensational hopes. It finds men not altogether wise, or free from avarice, or void of ambition; only moderately energetic, and sometimes a little lazy if there be no spur to labour. The guild idea denies none of these undeniable facts; it is not more ambitious than to suggest an older system under which these weaknesses of men did not have such dominating sway.

It was written a moment ago that the guildsmen do not propose any radical changes, but the statement must be modified. For one radical change we do ask. That is, the most ruthless suppression of the centralizing autocracy and bureaucracy which have grown like an incubus in the national life. We do want Westminster and Whitehall deprived of their illegitimate powers over our lives. In other words, we ask for the deportation from our public life of those small groups of industrial moneylenders who control the aforesaid Westminster and Whitehall as if they were their private estate offices – which in truth they almost are.

Now, be it noted that however sudden this change might be (not that there is any likelihood of its being sudden), it would not be one of those reversals of human tradition to which reference was made above. Central tyranny has always been at the surface of human society. It is not denied that it has been of gigantic effect; it has strangled man times out of number. But it has always been imposed on him from above, from outside. It was never one of his traditions to be governed by bureaucrats. It was often his own tradition to choose a king, or even a hereditary royal house, but it is not (as maintained in the first chapter) a necessary function of a royal house to interfere with the self-government of its people. There were many kings long before people thought of tolerating any kingly rights over their private lives. The king's law, in the sense of an interference with his people's customs, is almost a new idea. So in sweeping away a great bulk of central law and central organization, we would be only sweeping away the things of the surface, leaving the human nature and its traditions beneath merely the freer because of the clearing above. Thus the guilds might rather be called reaction than revolution.

In demanding freedom from the weight of central government the guildsmen therefore are asking for merely a negative change. Even this they do not suggest should be too sudden; though "human nature" would not much suffer if it were, for it is not a part of human nature, except in a very secondary sense. But man is such a delicate growth that he cannot bear even to part with evil too suddenly. So the reform, or clearing away, of the system of central government may unfortunately be a somewhat slow process, and there is nothing in the evolution of the guild system which is not compatible with this. Just as the central government has gradually taken away local and industrial powers from the smaller organs of society, so it may perhaps gradually transfer them back.

On the internal side, the process by which a trading company of today became a guild of tomorrow, might be a slow development. Sharing of profits might be followed by the natural sequence of sharing in the responsibility of making those profits, namely, co-operation in the management. Co-operative management would naturally lead sooner or later to an entirely democratic basis for the whole industry; that is, to an equality of power and profits between all the members. And there one would have the guild already made, to be fitted into the social organism as soon as the whole community had the wit to use it. But note how gradual all this will be: never quicker than the capacity of the members for the next step. If the members are ready, then the process of change may be as quick as they like. Until they are ready, quickness would not lead to success – but to disaster. The guildsmen will not be slow, unless for the very good reason that they cannot be quick. The system is not recommended because it may be slow, but just because no human social idea has ever yet succeeded in being quick. By all means make quickness an ideal to strive for, but let us not mistake an ideal for an accomplishment.

D. The Education of the Workers

The last section, suggesting that the possibility of advance depends on the capacity of the individuals for taking the next step, leads on naturally to the further point that the guild system is also based on the soundest educational principles. Insofar as every member of a guild will finally have a voice in its management, to that extent every guild will be a technical school wherein the members can learn every side of their craft, from its elementary processes, to its complex managerial problems.

When one arrives at questions of practical trade and industry the atmosphere breathed is altogether different from the vague sentimentality of political and bureaucratic life. In industry, one is driven to face facts; the chief business of the politician is to avoid them. It is by no means the least of the guild virtues that it will bring back our public life to the region of hard facts. It will teach the citizen that there is no more useful public work than the production of something useful – it may be a poem or a potato. That idea once grasped, the citizen will then realize that there is only one path to the production of the useful; to wit, the precise knowledge of the best method of producing it. It is hard to exaggerate the difference such a conception of fact and knowledge would make in the life of a society.

With our public life based on the practical production of national wealth there would be some considerable hope of purifying it. Once allow a man to discuss that misty shadow called a "political ideal," and the High Courts of Justice and all their judges cannot tie him down to a definite statement or a bindable promise. When this confirmed wriggler goes further and discusses a dozen diverse and usually inconsistent political ideals at the same time, little wonder that the elector, in a moment of admiration, thinks he has been addressed by a superman. Whereas it was only a first-class conjurer, with the added qualities of an experienced salesman. If we would get rid of the charlatan in public life, there is no surer way than to discuss facts instead of sentiments.

One very valuable result will be to convince the labour movement that if it desires to control the wealth of the country, on behalf of the workers, there is no shortcut to victory. The workers will not control the wealth until they know how to produce it themselves without the assistance of the capitalist. The reason why the plutocrat has his men in the hollow of his hand is because the workers are not in a position to step into his place and conduct the industry without him. What other reason can there be? A few shillings per head from the working class would quickly raise the capital necessary to make a trial of democratic management in any industry. Why do they not raise it, and become their own masters? Mainly because they have not sufficient knowledge of the processes of their trade, either on the technical productive side or on the financial and commercial side.

The guild system would tend to give the workers just this insight that is now their chief lack. They have the main key to the industrial position in their hands, because they alone can provide the labour. They surrender what might be an impregnable position to their masters, mainly because they are not able to use their labour themselves. Until they make up their minds to master the whole knowledge of their crafts, from top to bottom, so long will labour be helpless – and one might almost add, that it will deserve its fate, and the plutocrats will almost deserve their victory. If it were only as a matter of education, it would be wise of the workers to accept that instalment of reform called co-partnership and co-management. In practice, even co-partnership would inevitably carry with it the first steps in co-management. It is hard to understand why such a first step is so bitterly resisted by some of the men who profess to write for the working class. If the ambition and the dignity of labour are in danger of being so easily satisfied by a concession of this kind, then they must be of a poor, sickly quality. A quite trivial knowledge of history and human nature would teach these timid souls that nothing so spurs on ambition as the beginning of success. It is not the downtrodden who rebel easily; it is those who have breathed the fine scent of victory in their nostrils and clamour for more. Perhaps, after all, ambition may be a poor thing; it may have the elements of sickness. But, certainly, so long as we call ambition a virtue, then let us realize that its fires are fed by success. Even the modest heights of co-partnership and co-management, and the similar homely virtues of the Whitley Reports[37] and its kind, may do much good, and certainly cannot do any harm, unless the workers are ready to acknowledge that they are so easily duped.

E. The Democratic Distribution of Power and Wealth

There are those whose ultimate object in desiring the guild system is that they are eager for the triumph of democracy over autocracy, for the victory of the poor over the plutocrat. They have seen how bureaucracy is so easily captured by the men in possession, and so hardly to be used by the poor for their own defence. The guild system, as already discussed, is obviously a good plan for increasing the production of wealth and avoiding the present waste and inefficiency. As a rational business system, it could stand on that merit, and win easily. But it is theoretically possible for the guilds to make wealth for the plutocrats. However, in practice that will be impossible. It may be regarded as a certainty that the adoption of the guild system will be a triumph of the many poor over the few very rich.

The problem of equality of wages within a guild has already been mentioned in the chapter on self-management. There is no reason to suppose that even the most democratic of guilds will refuse to give higher wages to those who do higher work. Certainly, equality of reward is not an inherent part of the system, though it is certainly an ideal for the perfect man. If the promise of increased reward is the most satisfactory way of encouraging human beings to do increased work, then sensible human beings will so act—principles and other lofty things notwithstanding. But apart from the rewarding of special merit, there will undoubtedly be a general levelling of the wealth of the community. Smart bankers and popular novelists will no longer be judged worthy of the grotesque sums which they seize from the public revenue. They may both continue to receive more than the modest citizen who can only sweep the streets, but the man with a passion for finance or a taste for literature will be tempted to display his peculiar abilities for something far less than his spoils of today. They will be content with as much fame and rather less fortune. The "leisured class" (our polite term for the lazy class) will, of course, disappear. For there will be no guild to contain them. If they have any of the qualities of the wandering minstrel or the clown, they may find a quiet backwater of life in those Bohemian circles whose inhabitants have often enough good taste to prefer happiness and a clean conscience to success—for ambition, after all, is really a plutocrat's virtue at the best, and most of his virtues are vices. One hopes there will be room for many idle dreamers in the guild state, but they must pay for that proud position by sacrificing the bulk of their incomes.

The guild system will inevitably put power into the hands of the majority—just as inevitably as the Bureaucratic system has put power into the hands of a very few—and it would be ridiculous to imagine for one moment that the possession of such a power will not naturally result in a fairer sharing of the national wealth. But it will not be an absolute equality, as already stated; and this, because, first, it is exceedingly difficult to get perfect equality, and secondly because no one will very insistently demand it. As to the difficulty, it will, for example, be no easy task to ensure that one guild will not receive a greater reward than another. It might be done at the cost of an infinite amount of bookkeeping. But would it be worth it? It will, one hopes, be a deep characteristic of the guild idea, that nothing will be held worth much bookkeeping – which was mainly invented for usurers and misers, and not for honest workmen. The people who insist so much on the need for perfect equality of wages are just those who attach too much importance to the factor of material reward. A man who is interested above all else in his work will not be unutterably depressed if another receives a rather greater reward for his efforts. That would only annoy a moneylender.

F. The Healing of Social Wounds

The average worker will not be content until he gets better pay and more dignity, and he is right in refusing any other terms. A clever plutocracy might give him better pay, but the worker does not attach the same absolute importance to pay that his more vulgar masters do. He must also have his human dignity preserved. It is in granting this that the guild system offers more than any other, whether it be bureaucracy, plutocracy, monarchy or aristocracy. None of these gives the same chance to merit and self-respect, that would alone be recognized in the more intimate and more technical circle of the guilds.

Such are some of the secondary principles and effects which seem naturally to follow the three main principles of the guild state. It is one of the virtues of that system that we are not at all sure what will follow it. A firm belief that human beings, freed from external coercion, will keep within the sane limits of their human traditions compels one to look to the past for the main outlines of the future. The future will probably be only a dignified improvement of the past, at the best, and it will be a very good best if it merely succeeds in escaping from the present. It is a little difficult to realize that what we imagine to be the deep-rooted character of the present system is not deep or rooted at all, but merely the floating debris, cast up as the wreckage of an appalling social disaster, but, after all, only one wrecked vessel out of the vast fleets of humanity that are still sailing safely to port. We in England have seen more of the catastrophe than have others, undoubtedly; unless we except those other two great nations which have, like ourselves, bartered their souls for material wealth: to wit, the United States of America and Germany. There are plenty of evils in the world, elsewhere; but perhaps it is only the people of the United States and Germany and ourselves, who, having wandered so far from decent human traditions, will have much trouble to return again to sanity.

THE COAT OF ARMS OF
A 15TH-CENTURY DUBLIN
CRAFT GUILD

CHAPTER VI

RELATIONS BETWEEN GUILDS AND STATE

AVING ASSUMED that organization by function – that is by producing and trading and professional guilds – is the main basis of the healthy state, at the first glance it might seem that the whole ground of national government is thereby covered. It might be considered that since every citizen of a state should be engaged in work of some kind or another, therefore he would be represented in one of the guilds. Theoretically that argument is very reasonable; link all the guilds together in a national assembly or parliament, and we would have the ideal state as a complete whole. But for the first stages, at any rate, there would be all sorts of little nooks and crannies left outside, and hundreds of quite useful citizens who would not be clearly sortable into appropriate guilds. Besides, although the guild would represent the man who was a member of it, he would be continually dealing with other guilds, both as a producer and as a buyer of their wares. The ordinary man would have two definite sides even as a member of a very complete guild state. He would be producer in particular and citizen in general. It is the analysis of his position as citizen that is the subject of this chapter.

It is obvious that we are on much more indefinite grounds than in the previous part of the argument. The guild, rightly or wrongly, has been taken as a fixed point in the state, as the essential centre of it. It therefore follows that any other national factors must be relative to this fixed central point. Having determined that the guild is essential, all other ideas are merely matters of expediency and convenience. They have to fit in with the main idea of organization by function. It is unwise to be too dogmatic on this subject of the relation of the state to the guilds, for it is very difficult to be certain what form that relationship will take. It may be found that a very slight state structure will suffice to support the guild organs. On the other hand, it is quite possible that a very substantial state will be necessary. Anyhow, it is certain that in the beginning at least the state will have to do much which later may be done by the guilds, without external assistance.

A large part of the early problem will be of a negative kind. The first object of the reformers will be to get rid of that blighting, corrupting, influence of central control which at present prevents healthy action. The first thing to do with the state is not to give it new powers, but rather to take away those illegitimate powers which it should never have possessed. The political reform of the present governing system is necessarily a part of the guild problem for the same reason that one drains a marsh before starting to build upon it. One could no more expect the present politicians to reform our society than one could hope that a committee of the Stock Exchange would revive good taste in art.

The central state may play a great part under the guild system, but it is quite certain that this cannot happen in the lifetime of the present political constitution. We at least owe a debt of gratitude to the present politicians for showing us so clearly all that must be avoided. Whatever the central government organ may be, it certainly cannot be a parliament controlled by the clique who masquerade under the two-party system. We may eventually find a parliamentary system of government by Lords and Commons a good thing, but we know that government by a small group of political intriguers is an utterly bad thing, and has very little to do with Lords or Commons, or, indeed, with representative government at all.

The party system is mainly based on a ridiculous rule by which a government can dissolve a parliament at its discretion; in other words, on its power of dragging down in its fall the whole Cabinet and all the members of the Commons. So long as a whole parliament will cease unless the government supporters obey the autocratic orders of its Cabinet; in other words, so long as a government can force its supporters to vote as it commands, so long will our political system be a laughing-stock. As it exists today, if the members of the Commons refuse to obey, there is a government defeat, which usually means a dissolution. How many men are there in the House of Commons who would not rather sacrifice their consciences than their seats? It may be replied that until our politicians have honesty, any system will fail. But at least we can see to it that we do not give every encouragement to political adventurers. If the House of Commons were given a fixed life of, say, five years, and a direct vote of censure, asking for the government's resignation, were necessary before a Cabinet could appeal to the country; then a vote in the House could be free of all motives except the desire to assist or defeat the precise question in dispute at the moment. Then, again, why should a whole government fall just because a majority of the members of the Commons disapprove of one clause in one bill? Here again is a system which surely was deliberately designed to make a slave of the individual in order to strengthen the men who control. Each member of a government should be chosen (by the House of Commons) for his definite work; if he fails to retain the approval of the House, and a bill introduced by him is defeated, then let him, and him alone, retire from office. There is no reason in Christendom why a whole Cabinet should fall with him. There will be political corruption until every vote in the Commons can be freely given on its own merits. The party system is planned to prevent that introduction of common sense.

Let us now consider the necessary functions of a central government in a guild state. We must first realize that the guilds will absorb a vast amount of the work which at present comes under the control of the central departments. Such affairs as education and public health will be sorted out to the various guilds of education, guilds of doctors, and sanitary engineers concerned. If the doctors and the teachers cannot give us good health and sound education, then it is clear that we have got to a *cul-de-sac*[38] in nature, and it would be merely childish to hand over the impossible to politicians and bureaucrats. That would be making the impossible also intolerable. Once accept the guild system, and it follows that the central government is relieved of a vast bulk of its functions; or, at least, it will assign these to the guilds to execute them as its agents.

With all the functions of production, in its widest sense, transferred to the guilds, what will remain in the hands of the central administration? It is dangerous to be dogmatic on this point. As suggested above, there is no great principle to guide us; it is rather a matter of practical convenience. We will leave everything to the state which the guilds cannot conduct with greater skill as professionals.

Take the case of foreign affairs. It is a little difficult to think of a Guild of Diplomats. It might even need no little argument to persuade decent persons, under the new conditions, to allow themselves to bear the name of a profession that has now no sweet flavour in the mouths of most people who desire common honesty and common sense. The men who allowed England to drift unwarned into the Great War did not know their trade; the men who allowed themselves to be outwitted by the crudities of German blood and thunder did not know the rudiments of their craft. But one does not "produce" international treaties in the ordinary sense of the word. It will be one of the few matters where the wishes of the public will overrule the professional advice of the diplomatic draftsmen. We have had too much of diplomats with a free hand; the free hand might be all right, of course, if it had gone with average brains and the honour of the state, but so far, diplomats have considered the interests of a small class – as often as not from sheer stupidity; when honest themselves, they have rarely had the courage to show it. Anyhow, there will probably not be a Guild of Diplomacy. The matter will be left under the control of a body of secretaries directly controlled, as at present, by a minister or committee of the central assembly.

As long as we are vulgar barbarians, we shall continue to waste our national wealth on an army and a navy. These, again, can scarcely be guilds; it would not be convenient, for many reasons, to allow them to be self-managing. War as a profession would naturally only attract a very inferior class of mind, as it has usually done in the past – with many brilliant exceptions, of course. The ordinary professional soldier would be something very different from the many great men who rushed to support their country and their principles in a temporary peril. While, here again, we could scarcely ask an Army Guild to "produce" us a victory, as we would ask the bootmakers to produce boots. So the Army and Navy, like the diplomatic service, will remain as the directly controlled servants of the state. But this problem, one hopes, is only a very temporary one; at the worst they will have vanished from civilization within a few decades. It is in the nature of a gigantic joke that the professional soldier has so often prided himself on saving civilization, forgetting that had it not been for the generals and the diplomats, there would have been very few dangers from which to be saved.

Having dismissed some of the unimportant sides of central government, there remains those functions that are really essential. There will be under the guild system, as at present, a vast mass of legislation that will be common to the whole nation. Such, for example, as the laws laying down a national minimum. That is, the united citizens will decide that there shall be a limit below which the standard of life must not fall. There will probably be a minimum wage; a maximum for working hours; standard rules for health conditions. Whether it will be the duty of each guild to support its unemployed and pay its own old-age pensions; whether, in short, each trade must bear its own burdens as well as its profits; all that is a matter of detail, the result of which will not be known until it is settled. It is just one of those cases where a good deal of time is wasted in discussions of theory; it is largely a matter of practical expediency to be decided when the moment arrives.

The criminal laws, the law of contracts and torts, will require common control by the whole state. But it is quite possible that, just as one very usual rule of the medieval guilds ordered all civil disputes between members first to be referred to the guild, so it may well be under the revived system; leaving the state judges to deal only with appeals by the losing party who will not accept the decision of his fellow members; and cases of crime, and civil actions between litigants who are not members of the same guild. But these, once more, are matters of expediency, and they may reasonably be decided in several different ways. In brief, so far as it can be generalized, there will be departments and officials representing the central state to settle many of those common concerns of the citizens which are settled by the state today. But it must not be forgotten that it will be the continual tendency of a well-educated society to withdraw power from the hands of the state, rather than to add thereto. The Fabian[39] and bureaucratic theory that civilization means an increasing functioning by the state, is, of course, a comparatively old-fashioned opinion. The more civilized a man is, the less he requires instruction from policemen and government clerks. The whole guild theory rests on the theory that man should be his own governor—for the commonsense reason that the professional governors are rarely any good at their job, and because man when too much governed becomes a worm—and worms do not interest anyone but scientists.

There is one all-important function of the central state which directly concerns the guilds. The creator of the greater medieval guilds, in the legal sense, was the Crown, who granted the charter under which the guildsmen claimed their power. It seems probable that the modern guilds will be created in a very similar manner. One imagines that the grant of a charter will work out in some such manner as follows. A group of traders or producers will voluntarily link themselves together and ask the state to recognize them as a guild. It may be that they are discontented with the guild in which they have hitherto worked; or perhaps the old guild has grown too large in membership or area, and requires rearrangement into smaller units; or there may be a new trade or process involved. Probably the petition for the charter will first be referred to the existing guild organizations, as represented either by the units in the neighbourhood concerned, or by the larger guild assemblies which, as suggested in an earlier chapter, are almost certain to be formed in each industry or trade for common consultation. This body would naturally, as competitors, as a general rule put the case against the petition; if the justice of it were acknowledged by its non-trading rivals, there would be little more to be said, except the formal grant of a charter by the state.

But it is more likely that the petition, and the case against it drawn up by the rival guilds of the same trade, would be referred to a department representing the united community. This might be one appointed by the national government, and it would then be a kind of Board of Trade. Or it might be referred to a committee representing the united Congress of the Guilds – which might be the form ultimately taken by the central state. The main object would be to find some procedure that would give the community as a whole the right to decide whether the proposed new guild should be granted a monopoly, either absolute or partial, in the trade of its district. The exact way of carrying that object into practice might vary within a large range of methods.

There is another side to this granting of a charter. The initiative may come from a body of the consumers, who may petition the sanctioning authority either to grant a new charter, or even to withdraw or revise one already granted. For any number of reasons they may be dissatisfied with the guild already supplying their neighbourhood. They may think it good that there should be more competition, or a new want may have sprung up. A growing village may need a building guild of its own, instead of merely absorbing the spare time of the builders centred in the nearest town, and if growing in houses, that would suggest the need for many other new guilds to supply the dwellers therein. In the need of such a petition, from the ordinary man in the street, there is an indication of the necessity of providing some easy procedure whereby the ordinary man will have a real voice in this vital question in his everyday life. One can imagine a fairly democratic nation that might allow the condition of the West Indies to be settled by a Foreign or Colonial Office without very much interference, but a democracy that could not be the deciding factor in choosing its butcher and builder, its baker and candlestick maker, would be a contradiction in terms. Liberty, like its sister Charity, begins at home.

It is perhaps in this right to control industry by charters that we find the most vital function of the state. It will certainly be its most delicate problem. If done successfully, it will solve a very large majority of the difficulties of public affairs; if it fails, then we shall be no better off than we are today; but it is pleasant to remember that even utter failure can scarcely make things worse than they are now. It will be noted that although the words "control by charter" are used, yet the whole gist of the solution is to put the real control in the hands of the guilds themselves. The guild charter merely decides to whom that right of control shall be granted. Yet even when granted, it will be on stated terms; it will be a contract between the guildsmen and the state, which will be revisable if those terms are infringed.

In some cases, but probably not many, there will be granted an absolute monopoly; that is, the guild will be the only body entitled to conduct the specified trade within the specified district. Generally speaking, there will probably be more than one charter in action at the same place and time. In other words there will be competition. Whether there shall be this competition will largely be in the hands of the inhabitants of the area, who will have, as already observed, the right to petition for a new guild, and representation at the local public inquiry which would be held before a charter was granted. This inquiry would, or should be, perhaps, the most important function in the life of a citizen. If the rights of democracy broke down here, then they assuredly would fail throughout the social structure. Anyhow, the wit of man can scarcely hope to suggest a procedure more democratic than a local court, open to all as hearers and as witnesses. If democracy fails here, then failure is inevitable and it must accept its defeat. It will not be its first defeat, alas!

The terms of the charter will probably include a time limit, or power of revision after a trial of the capacity of the guild to do its work. There will also be a defined geographical area in which the guild may operate. Further, of course, there will be defined its industrial area; that is, the charter will only give permission to conduct a specified trade, just as a company's articles of association carefully define its trading scope today. The general standards of life laid down in the national legislation will naturally be assumed in the charter, but more precise conditions may be included to meet the special conditions of any trade. For example, the state may decide to impose special precautions in the case of coal mines, though it is scarcely conceivable that the miners themselves will sanction internal regulations which endanger their lives. Indeed, when we remember that the complete guilds will be both independent and democratic, we will realize that a vast mass of central legislation will naturally become obsolete. The guildsmen will be their own protectors.

The financial clauses will be the most important terms of the charter. It seems possible that a main element of national taxation may be the "rent" that the state will charge to the guild in return for its charter. In the case of a coal mine there will be rent, in the ordinary sense, for the use of the mine itself, which of course under any modern system would be the property of the state. That principle has already practically been accepted by a majority of the nation. The same ordinary rent clause would apply to agricultural guilds, for land undoubtedly is already on the verge of becoming public property. This does not rule out the possibility of leasing it out to peasant proprietors with hereditary rights for their descendants. These peasants could then form guilds if they chose. For again, one must insist that there will not necessarily be more rigidity or fixed formality in a guild state than there was under the older guild economy of the Middle Ages. Whether guild or no guild even will be a matter of expediency in each case. So in the case of most guilds there would be rent payable for some premises or land involved in their work. It may be a factory building or a brickyard, or a golf guild might desire to rent links.

But in a broader sense, "rent" would probably be payable under the charter: that is, the guild would be asked to pay a tax in return for its right to the partial or absolute monopoly of trade. This tax might be annual and heavy enough to represent its income tax. Or it might be a simple fixed charge, a revenue stamp, as it were, on the charter, sufficient to discourage any frivolous applications from a body which did not mean serious business. It might even be held good to put the charter up to public competition, to be granted to the guild (otherwise held satisfactory) which would pay the largest sum for the privilege. This might be just one of those ways of encouraging a healthy competition, in distinction from the sheer anarchical scramble of today.

Then again, the charter might lay down conditions concerning the prices to be charged to the consuming public. For example, a fixed price might be specified for the coal produced by a mining guild. In that case it probably would be so fixed, for it is fairly easy to standardize it. But in the case of a bootmakers' guild, the price would not be so easily determined, for it would vary with size and quality, so much more than coal; therefore the price of boots might be more conveniently left to the healthy competition of rival guilds and the public demand. In the case of an excessive price, there would soon be petitions from new guildsmen or complaining buyers. Nevertheless, it might be possible for the state to learn from the experience of all its guilds what was the standard cost of production. With this evidence at its disposal, we might go back to that highest moment in the history of industrial ethics when, as throughout the Middle Ages, there was a "fair price," which was the cost of production plus a fair return for the producer's labours. The cost of production was the foundation of the standard, and it is the only honest and rational standard that can be applied.

So far it has been assumed that this institution called the state, which is to have the power to grant or to refuse a charter of incorporation to a guild, is that rather pompous, old-fashioned thing as we know it today. It would be truer to say—as we do not know it today, for the clearest fact about the state is that it is not clear at all, but very mysterious. If it were not mysterious, if we knew it as it is, our governors, who are our state in real life, could not exist beyond a matter of hours. The only hope for a modern political statesman is that he should remain unknown by his subjects. For this reason, its impalpable mysteriousness, the modern state is suspected by honest men, who trust light more than darkness. The rebellion against the centralized state has begun, and it would be ridiculous to assume finally—as has been done in this chapter hitherto—that the state of the future will continue to bear the same form as in the past.

Already there is much talk of a federated United Kingdom instead of a single body represented by one parliament. Quite apart from the question of Irish Home Rule, there is a suggestion that Scotland and Wales should also have separate parliaments dealing with their own affairs. A Scotch Home Rule Bill has already been introduced in the Commons. Some would go still further and ask what Lancashire and Sussex have in common that they should be asked to interfere in each other's business by sharing the same assembly at Westminster. Why should the desires of industrial Lancashire be judged by the fishermen and farmers and lodging-house ladies of Sussex? There was a time when England was divided into at least seven substantial kingdoms; and still earlier, our present southern counties represented more or less distinct units of government. As most old things are better than anything new, it appears every day more probable that a reaction against overcentralization will make us retrace our steps in national history. By the time the guilds have arrived and they have to contest their power with the state, they will find a very different institution than the one we see today.

Thus, if federation follows, the guilds of Wales may not be compelled to come to Westminster to procure their charters. Indeed, Wales is a very good case for the new federation. It is really a distinctive unit, both racially and economically. We have no right to discuss subjects like the Welsh Church, in the sense of overriding the decision of the Welsh people. And certainly Wales interferes far too much with us. But it is in no spirit of revenge that we offer Mr. Lloyd George to his countrymen for internal consumption. If Wales, as well as Ireland and Scotland, were separate political units, then it would no longer be a Board of Trade in Whitehall which would be the creator of guilds, but a more local Board either at Dublin, or Edinburgh, or the Welsh capital. As there would be, probably, still a United Kingdom Parliament, the question arises whether there would be any appeal to the central Board against the decision of the local body. The chances are that it would be held unnecessary. What more of the case could be known at the centre than was known on the spot? It is a delusion that a better judgement is obtained as one goes higher and further away. It is one of those remarkably insolent fictions invented by bureaucrats, and it is one of their most palpable untruths. So there will probably be no ordinary procedure contracted whereby the decision of a local Board can be overridden by a centralized one, short, of course, of some extraordinary resolution by the United Parliament asking the case to be transferred on appeal.

But there is still another alternative to consider in this all-important procedure of granting charter monopolies to the guilds. It is possible that in the first instance, at least, the sanctioning authority may be a more or less local body representing the present municipal or county councils. Perhaps the municipal council will again be, as it was often in the Middle Ages, practically the united guilds; if so, they would be a convenient body to which the granting of the charters could be referred, at least in the first instance. If the council and the burgesses could not between them judge the facts on their merits, then the case would indeed be a difficult one, and more suitable for pulling straws than further argument. The county council might do the same work in all cases lying outside the greater municipal areas, where the problems are naturally somewhat different.

In short, it is necessary to think of the state as something very different, in form, from the centralized machine it is today. Without insisting on any desire or necessity to go back, yet there is little doubt that under the guild system the state will be much nearer what it was when the guilds were so supreme in the Middle Ages. There are some people, of course, who will object to "going back" on principle. Some people's principles are so rigid that they would rather do the wrong thing with them than do right without them. It is surely a matter of fact in this case. If the medieval system gave better results then, and would give equally good results now, then, indeed, why not follow that fact to its logical conclusion. A moment's consideration will surely convince most people that a continuation of going forward in our present direction is a far more terrible vision than going back, or sideways, or in any new dimension of space whatever. The medievalists are often called dreamers, still more unkindly critics use the word sentimentalists. There are some of us who will continue to prefer the quiet of dreams and sentiments to the reckless gamble of going forward as our critics are themselves going today. There is some advantage in being a dreamer if it makes us see the facts. What is the matter with so many hard-headed businessmen and politicians is that they cannot recognize them; their heads are so hard they cannot feel the impact.

The medieval state paid great respect to the city, and it is probable that under a decentralized system, it will again take an honourable place. Winchester may again become the capital city of a minor governing unit that has many independent powers of its own, without being compelled to refer to the main state on a hundred points of law and administration where reference cannot be a help, but rather a hindrance. Winchester and its county will not claim this independence from any stubborn conviction that it ought to be independent, and it will not be granted its freedom from centralization because of some vague instinct for liberty—though there are few instincts that are sounder. Its independence will exist just because, as a matter of practice, it will be agreed that local independence works more satisfactorily than central bureaucracy. Affairs will not be brought to London, for the very good reason that they can be better completed at Winchester. It is only the present-day politicians who are sentimental and theoretical on such matters; the guildsmen refuse to be swayed by anything except very solid arguments.

To take another example, such a county as Lancashire would have admirable excuses for claiming to exist as a minor and semi-independent administration, without the necessity of continually stopping its work in order to explain to Whitehall what Whitehall ought to allow the people of Lancashire to do. That complicated process is so remarkably like the tedious ceremony by which Louis the Fourteenth was hindered from putting on his clothes in the morning in order that a few dozen courtiers might hold honourable post about his person. He might have been handed his shirt by the first noble lord, but it had to go through many departments of the Court before it reached its owner's back. And that is exactly what happens with a bureaucracy and a centralized state. Its object is not to get its work done quickly, but to supply many people with offices.

But all these theoretical divisions of the country into smaller units must be considered entirely as a matter of practical convenience, not as a rigid principle. The principle merely lays down the rather obvious rule that one should never carry a problem to a geographical or intellectual Whitehall if it can be settled without the trouble of carrying it anywhere. That is scarcely a principle; it is only common sense. But the application of this principle is a matter which can only be decided in each case as it arises, and on its own merits. Lancashire may be a sound unit, whereas Westmoreland and Durham may be very bad ones. One can easily conceive that the agricultural interests of Norfolk and Suffolk and Lincolnshire and Essex might make them well rid of the suburban voters of the London district. But all these problems must be left to gradual enlightenment; and only after the guild system has sorted out the nation into its fundamental parts. That is the chief point to bear in mind: the guilds are the real dividing line; all other subdivisions or centralizations are only questions of practical expediency.

But however far the decentralization may be carried, there will always be something left over that will be better settled by the united state – for the good reason that it concerns the whole rather than the part. There will be broad questions of policy – very little of administration perhaps – which can only be settled by national collaboration, just as there will be still broader questions which will need international decision. So that, sooner or later, it will be necessary to face the problem of the structure of the central organ of government. That it should stand just as it is today is obviously impossible. The parliamentary system has become a byword of contempt, and a model of inefficiency. Nobody imagines that the seven hundred odd men in the House of Commons are the most patriotic, the most unselfish, the most honest, and the best men for their work. Of course they have got an impossible job, which would be mismanaged by archangels, but it would be hard to find a worse selection. A system that could choose such a weird jumble of members is self-condemned without much argument.

It seems clear, as we have already discussed, that the first element of a sound representative system is that the electors should have intimate knowledge of the opinions and character of their candidates, and that they should also have some real knowledge of the subjects on which a decision is asked. Without these two elements, the elections must be a matter of sporting chances, which might as well be settled more cheaply with the dice-box. It has been suggested in this essay that the personal qualifications of a candidate can scarcely be gained elsewhere than as a fellow worker in the intimate practice of the same daily work, which would also fulfil the second condition of knowledge of the subject, so long as it was only the problems of that trade. But how are we to choose a man who will decide, say, our relations with the Hottentots, when we have only the most remote idea what these people want or what they ought to have?

It would appear that we must give up in despair any ideal solution of this problem of finding the right parliamentary representatives. There will always be a large margin of chance. Politics will always tempt the adventurer, especially the man or woman who would otherwise find it difficult to make a living. The orator and the wire-puller will always have the best chance of beating the thinker and the honest man at the polls. As it will be always impossible for the electors to have an expert knowledge of every subject that arises during an election, that factor of the problem must often take its chance. It remains, therefore, to cling to the first principle that at least the electors may know their candidates.

If a man is chosen for his honesty and shrewd common sense, he will be found fairly adequate to give the reasonable and honest vote on most occasions. No system will be foolproof or knave-proof. If knowledge of our candidates is thus our main hope, perhaps it may be found necessary to sweep away the area representation altogether, and elect the members of the central parliament on the basis of the guilds. Each guild would return its member or share him with its neighbouring guilds. But as the number of guilds would make the assembly too large for practical purposes, it is possible that the united delegates of a whole industry might make the election. Though here again, the knowledge of the candidate would be rather slight. Or an alternative system would be for quite small areas, say a parish, to choose primary electors who would then group together in, say, county areas and choose the members. There are obvious defects, but, as already admitted, all systems seem to be weak somewhere. The whole idea of representation is a mere concession to the unfortunate fact that we cannot be in a dozen places at one time.

It may therefore be that we shall have to choose the best of the defective ways of central election, and comfort ourselves with the thought that in the guild state we shall have removed as many subjects as possible from the power of the central machine. And by hitting at the party system as hard as possible we shall do much to make what remains of centralization as little dangerous as must be. Besides, no government will be wiser or more honest than its electors. There is no perfect solution of the representative system except by first finding an educated electorate. The wiser the voter, the less often will he choose a fool or a rogue; and until he is wise there is little use our crying for the moon. For we will not get it.

THE COAT OF ARMS OF THE
DUBLIN MERCHANTS GUILD
OF THE TUDOR PERIOD

CHAPTER VII

A Guildsman's Philosophy of Life

AVING ENTICED THE READER to bear with the fore-going essay on the guilds, tempting him by a plea that the social machinery of the state is a vital matter in human affairs, the time has now come for a con-fession. These questions of social machinery, these details of economic and political constitutions, have been altogeth-er overrated. There are intellectual freaks who sometimes emerge from our educational system (usually from the honours schools at the universities), who imagine that man will save his soul by the infinite collecting and studying of political constitutions. They tabulate them and arrange them in their libraries, as wiser men collect and pin butterflies. They would seem to believe that the fate of man hangs on the thread of whether he be a proportional-rep-resentation man or a mere voter after the old-fashioned Victorian manner. They get passionate in defending the federal state against the confederates. They imagine, in short, that man clings to social salvation by the hair of a political constitution. There are political dreamers and economic professors who collect constitutions and regulations with the simple enthusiasm of schoolboys collecting postage stamps – and, for all the results one can discover, with the equal satisfaction of a harmless and innocent curiosity. For wheth-er man has one civic constitution or another seems ultimately of as little importance as when Brazil changes the colour of its postage stamps.

The chief fault of the learned is that they have no sense of pro-portion, which is a high philosophic quality usually reserved for the simple. Education is too often an overbalancing of the values of life; the scholar so persistently sees one thing at a time – usually the wrong one. It is therefore urgent that we should get the social machinery of the guild state in its proper proportion against the background of life as a whole. It is not the centre of the picture, but merely one part of it, however essential. Until we know what we want life to be, we shall never be quite sure whether we ought to have the guilds, or how we should use them when we get them. They are not an end in themselves, but merely a means. Reformers so continually harp on the machinery and forget the men for whose use it was made. Man is the centre of human society, and the machinery is only good if it suits his ultimate purposes in life.

What the guildsman must grasp is that these proposals go no further than the mere mechanism of social anatomy; and without some understanding of what he finally intends to do, he may easily grasp the form of the guilds and find that the spirit has escaped. One can imagine a community led by university professors and constitution collectors building themselves a guild state – as architects might build an imitation Greek temple or a sham Gothic church – and then wondering why everything remained much as it was before. Or worse still, not realizing they had never really desired anything new, except some new machinery to fit the latest pattern in their constitution album.

The guildsman, if he is anything more than another sort of political adventurer, wants many things much more fundamental than new machinery. He wants new results. But unfortunately this is not always his aim. There are some who do not object to the present political and industrial system because it is radically wrong, from its very roots to its most rotten fruit; they think it is merely badly managed. Their intellectual and artistic outlook is almost precisely that of the sympathetic countess in Balzac[40] who on seeing a poorly clad peasant boy exclaims, "Tu n'as donc pas de mère!"[41] She thought that if he only had a mother all would be well. She was like the man who imagines that the present system will be all right when incomes are more equally distributed. He does not, for example, desire to abolish the centralized factories; he merely wants them made clean and bright. He does not want to change the present social system, but only to tidy it. He wants

Lancashire to continue to produce cotton goods by the ten million yards, and Durham to dig coal by the million tons, and he will be delighted if Kent can be induced to follow their example. There are two classes of social reformers: those who are seeking a radical change, and those who belong to the same school as the young woman in the apron who flicks the dust off one chair in order that it may quietly settle down on another. Both schools may be entirely sincere; indeed, the most sincere are usually the dullest. But they have different philosophies of life, and until we know which is the right one, it is useless to start off aimlessly in any direction whatever. Social reform is not a game of blindman's buff.

The medieval system had one conception of life, and the modern system has another. We have the factory system now because a certain powerful group of men want something which is entirely different from the ideal of the average medieval man. The two conceptions can be summed up in a reasonable space; there is the ideal modern man, and the ideal man as the medievalists conceived him. One hopes to show that the former is a figment of diseased minds, and that the latter is the normal man, as he exists in a rational world. The antagonism between the two ideas may be put in various ways; for the moment it is important to make clear what precisely is the root difference which separates the guild school of reform from the modern state school.

What, then, do the champions of this modern state conceive to be the chief end of man? What is their ideal of life? The answer can only be gathered from the chaotic mass of evidence by which the system reveals itself. We can most easily judge of the modern man's ideals by the system he supports and strives to continue. It is a little difficult to know where to begin, for the main note of modern life is a rushing, roaring tumult of noise and rapid motion. To describe it from the life would be somewhat like trying to write a book of philosophy when seated in the din of a shipbuilding yard. The modern man seems to find some peculiar virtue in noise and movement. They appear to represent to his mind great natural forces which he associates with work and success. He is convinced that a great deal is happening in the world if there is a great noise. He is sure that progress is being made if somebody is going somewhere at a very rapid pace. He is convinced that there is more real energy in the world now that there are railway trains and trams and bicycles, instead of the old system of walking or riding in a cart. When the motorcar was invented, the modern man felt that the gods were kind indeed, for now he could travel all over the country at the same speed at which only the fixed railways could carry him before. He could cover a hundred miles of road, whereas before he could only do ten. He did not stop to ask himself whether he only saw one-tenth of the scenery. Having the quantitative mind, he was only concerned with total mileage.

The invention of the aeroplane was as strong wine to this enthusiast. All his newspaper writers put it into headlines and called it the "Conquest of the Air" in their biggest type. When London was being bombed every other night, there was a certain hesitation as to what was being conquered, but this balance was quickly restored when we had the best of this new game for modern men. That we should have a whole new element of space added to our possibilities for rapid travel, seemed too good to be true. It was apparently an inspiration to know that one could see so much more of the earth by flying over it so quickly—that it was impossible to see anything at all. It seems the crown of madness. It is pace for pace's sake. Of course there may be many reasons why it is better to get to Granada or Cairo rather than stop in London, and it may be good, therefore, to get there as soon as possible. But now we find this man of rapid passions developing a desire to fly to New York. But would any sane man want to go to such a place? Yes, the modern man wants to go there, for it sums up most of which he considered good in life. He may want a week or two at the seaside or in the country in the summer, but for the rest, give him New York every time, he will tell you. It seems a shame to put this ignominy so prominently on New York—but a hundred great cities would please him almost as well. So long as he can get speed, and noise, and dust, and as little fresh air as possible, the modern man will be content. He will be in his paradise.

But, by the very nature of his creed, no sooner has he arrived in one paradise than it is time to conquer another. Like Alexander,[42] he does not rejoice for what he has won, but weeps because there is nothing beyond. He wants to conquer and to rule everybody and everything, and above all else, he must be quick. His trusted philosopher is the journalist, that feverish mind that is lured to its folly by the latest evening telegram. Now the real news of the world cannot be discovered in a telegram, and wisdom can rarely be gleaned from it in time for the newspaper train. Wisdom is not the fancy of today or the fashion of tomorrow. But the modern man does not ask for wisdom; he wants opinion poured down his throat as quickly and as noisily as possible. So the daily newspaper has become the very expression of the intellect of this extraordinary byproduct of humanity.

This desire for speed is but the expression of the modern man's determination to value everything in terms of quantity instead of quality. If he can have two of anything, he feels himself infinitely better than if he only has one. He is unfortunately limited by one mouth, one stomach, by twenty-four hours to the day, and other ridiculous failings of a Nature that is so carelessly unambitious. But the modern man is not one to be dictated to by mere Nature. His whole life is one continual defiance of every law of it. He thinks Chicago is so many times better than Canterbury because there are so many times more people in it; and so many multiple times the possibility of making money in it. He thinks one nation is richer than another because its exports and imports are bigger. He thinks the British Empire is greater than the land of the Plantagenets because its square mileage has increased. He thinks a citizen of the United States must feel superior to the inhabitants of Denmark because it is possible to travel in a railway train longer in the States before reaching the boundary. He thinks that Mr. Jay Gould[43] and Mr. Carnegie[44] are more successful men than George Meredith[45] or Robert Grosseteste[46] because they have larger banking accounts. In his more genial moments he talks generously of the services of the clowns and singers and artists who amuse his moments of leisure; he is kind enough to murmur proverbs concerning the happinesses and virtues of contentment and poverty–but he doesn't really mean it; it is only a creed for those who have not wit enough to make a real success. In short, it is a Philosophy of Multiples; there is one test for everything–the multiplication table. That is his creed. His questions can only be answered in terms of quantity, of space, of velocity. He prefers the last part of the multiplication table to the beginning, for it talks about bigger numbers.

Now, the remarkable fact is that in the newspaper offices and government departments and business houses, where they imagine they know all the latest news, they really believe that this modern monstrosity is the normal man of today. They conceive of man as a heroic creature of energy who is continually asserting himself; ever restless to take the next step in human progress; always searching for something new, and imagining that the new is better than the old; always desiring to rule his fellows and to interfere with their lives as much as possible–for that is their conception of a great man. It is an astounding blunder in judgement. It no more corresponds to the facts of life than when a man in a moment of spiritual emotion sees two moons. The vast majority of the people of this world have no resemblance to this human motorbus, eternally rushing along the highways, smothered in the dust of its own energy, a thing of tumultuous noise and virile determination to get to its journey's end at all costs to itself or others. The journalist is deceived because he is himself of this weird mechanical creation, and likewise his friends. But it is the same sort of mistake that a duke would make if he imagined that all the other people in the world were dukes, with the corresponding number of duchesses. It is the same mistake that the orthodox historians make when they imagine that history has been made by politicians.

The normal man has no resemblance whatsoever to a motorbus. He is sane. He is exceedingly stable, and if he met his ancestors of the Middle Ages, or even of Greece and Rome, they would have much in common to discuss. There would be all those innumerable simple facts which make up the main life of the normal man. They would be more concerned with their daily occupations than with rushing along–either materially or mentally–somewhere else or nowhere in particular. Normal life is rest, not motion; quiet, not tumult; acceptance of what arrives at one's door, rather than the seeking of what is not there. The normal man lacks ambition; he is not anxious to make a great fortune, or to conquer, or to govern other people. It may be intellectual slackness or physical laziness, or, more probably, merely good taste and decent manners. Whatever may be the reason, he does not care to interfere with his neighbours. He does not want to govern them, and he dislikes being governed by them.

Perhaps that is the most fundamental civic quality of the average human being; this inability or disinclination to take a very active part in the business of governing. The politician may be very anxious to give the common people elaborate political constitutions that will confer on them many votes and many offices. But the normal man, rightly or wrongly, has never got very excited about his gifts. He will neither take a very great interest in the politician nor his programmes. The politicians, of course, have assumed that this was entirely owing to lack of education on the part of the common man, and great endeavours have been made to arouse him to more intellectual activity. But when one thinks over the matter more carefully, the suspicion is aroused that this placid ignoring of the political orator and his bag of tricks may be just one of those things that prove the sane wisdom of the common man. It may be his thoughtful judgement—the clinging traditions of his ancestral memory—that he got on fairly well in the past without either politician or political programmes, and that all those that he has voted for seem, on consideration, to have done him no particular good, and sometimes a great deal of harm. Anyhow, rightly or wrongly, the ordinary man as often as not will go to the poll only if he is carried there. He is not a political animal.

His ambition is of very modest proportion, desiring very moderate things, little inclined to self-assertion, peaceful; aroused to action only by the most persistent encouragement, provoked to resistance only by the most persistent tyranny. The freaks of humanity may demand a grouse moor in Scotland, a villa on the Riviera, a box at the opera, and dinner at the Ritz. The normal man is wonderfully content with very much less. Being very sane, and therefore unlike the modern man, he recognizes the limitations of facts. If everybody drank the wines of Tokay,[47] they could not last a day; the moors of Scotland would soon be surging with sportsmen and bare of grouse; the theatres would be all boxes, and a box in the gallery would be a quibble about terms. In short, the world would only be possible if the normal man kept his head and refused to become an abnormal freak. It is one of the great traditions of man to keep his head and heart steady, for without it the earth would become a reckless impossibility. If all succeeded, if all won fame, then both fame and success would lose their meaning. It would perhaps be possible to take in each other's washing—but each other's fame might become exceedingly boring.

But if the sane man has small ambition for greatness, he has a commendable desire to do his daily job with credit to himself. Man is by instinct a craftsman who likes his work. There was no strong economic coercive pressure in the Middle Ages, yet the craftsmen of that day built a thousand beautiful churches, and made ten thousand delightful wares. They were things that could only be done in the spirit of delight in doing them. But it is written in the history of the world that man in his natural condition is not content to get merely a bare living: he must always be throwing into his work an infinity of turns and twirls just because it delights him to do so, while the appeal to his sense of honesty and efficiency is generally certain of a due response. Man was an artist by nature, long before there were academy schools or technical colleges to teach him by classes. One of the pathetic struggles of today is to recover, by vast expenditure of public money on education, some of the artistic skill which the apprentice of the medieval days could pick up for the asking in every workshop. The deep traditions of the world would seem to have taught the normal man what is worth the doing and what is not worth it, and we find him willing, or even eager, to do his daily work if it is worthy of a decent creature. But he is very reluctant to trouble about all those matters which come under the head of political affairs.

There are the two types before us in very brief summary. The system of life which produces one must inevitably crush out the other. We must make up our mind which of the two we will have, for we cannot have both; it would be like placing a terrier and a rabbit in the same cage. At least it is certain that the guild state would threaten the destruction of the modern man. No one can suppose that this journalist's ideal could exist for long in an educated democracy; he would probably be expelled under one of the sanitary regulations, or somebody might lose his temper and hit him with an axe. But it must be seriously asked whether this modern man is either ideal, or necessary, or even possible as a permanent social institution. We have had it continually dinned into our ears that it is this striving, competitive, ambitious, self-assertive and noisy person who has made the progress of the world. But whither is this "progress" taking us? Quite clearly (if we are allowed to judge by results) it means more factories; more machines; more great towns and less country; more smoke, less sun; the workman will become more and more an automaton, a part of the machine; great art is to give place to great production; quantity of wealth is to be considered before its quality; man is to be turned into a scientific instrument for the production of goods; and the man who produces (or rather seizes) the most of them is to rule all the others who get less; government is to be performed by a class of trained bureaucrats who gather themselves into great capital cities as far away from popular control as possible; the individuality of the common man is to be reduced to a convenient standard; while the individuality of the nations will gradually disappear as they are gathered together into great states. Such seems to be the picture of this "progress," but, indeed, it is blurred; it half vanishes in the noise and dust and speed of its accomplishment. It is like a cinema that is working too fast.

But who are these who dictate the standards of life? We have sat silent too long while newspaper proprietors and university dugouts have splattered decent people with the grease of their ideal world, bred in their coal pits and factory yards. They have done their best to turn a beautiful earth into a noisy pigsty, and they have the cool audacity to expound it as a triumph of wisdom and taste. It is the dream of a company promoter, and they ask us to believe that it has the approval of science and philosophy. In the face of all the facts, they dare to claim that their modern system is a "progress" from the Middle Ages. Their argument is a continuous evasion of the truth.

There is room for a seasoned and well-balanced historian to work out with unimpeachable candour whether the modern society is really better than the old. He will have to consider, in historic detail, whether this much-belauded "energy" has not done as much harm as good; whether, if all men were "energetic," the world would be a paradise or a bear pit. Think of him calmly and searchingly: is this really the highest type of man? It is not a question for rhetoric, but for careful balancing of the facts. This historian would have to tell us if the people of England are really so much happier because their fathers had the energy to conquer an empire, or whether the whole idea of empire is merely a clever trick of the plutocrats and government officials who get their profits and salaries out of it. Even from their point of view, is it not a dangerous game? Rome was ruined by building an empire. If this modern ideal of energy and fierce striving is a good thing, then our late enemies, the Germans, should command our unmitigated respect.

This inquiring historian may emerge from his study with many astounding conclusions which are not yet considered orthodox in historical circles. He may decide, in cold blood and on the facts, that modern society has more noise than reason in its composition. On close examination it may be found that there is something essentially vulgar and immoral in this desire to rule other people. The normal man has not this craving; it is not merely that he lacks the energy, he generally also lacks the desire. There is an instinctive delicacy in the common mind which holds it back from the wish to coerce one's neighbours, whether it be for their good or ill. The historian may decide that government has in the main been the trade of an essentially vicious class; vicious, not in the sense of being personally dishonest or corrupt, but because it is fundamentally depraved to govern even well. The Prussian officer was such a crude type of the governing class that every one beyond reach of his sword could only shake with laughter. He was invented by the Fates for the enjoyment of music halls. But he was not the most vicious part of German government. The real danger was the efficient expert official. It sounded so reasonable to hold that a carefully trained class of administrators could most easily provide us with the best of governments in the best of worlds. Whether the German people are now satisfied that this perfect theory has worked out as perfectly in practice, is an interesting question. There are some people who think that what man must discover is the right kind of government. The strictly impartial historian may conclude that sometimes the best of governments have been the worst, because they have always meant so much the more of what is always bad. The German system of highly centralized and highly skilled government has proved disastrous just because it succeeded in doing the thing more efficiently than it had ever been done before in the history of the world. The danger of it was not that it failed, but that it succeeded. It turned the German people into a herd of well-governed sheep and moral degenerates, who could assassinate their neighbours, and think they were lofty-souled patriots when they drove in the bayonet.

The real heart of the guild idea is not a mere rearrangement of the social machinery, but an attempt to express a rearrangement of human ideals. It does not seek ideals that are merely pious hopes, but rather those that are the deepest traditions of the human race. It is the modern man who founds his system on sentiments; it is the guildsman, who is scientific and practical. He does not desire a social system based on the weaknesses of the few, but one which befits the strength of the many. Above all he does not judge that the final test of human society is whether it is best arranged for the greatest output of coal, or iron, or farthing newspapers; he does not value it by the speed of its trains or the size of its empires. He stubbornly insists that the supreme test of human society is man; that he is the central pivot on which all must revolve. When he is told that a factory system is necessary because that is the quickest way of producing boots or tin cans, he asks the simple question: Is it the quickest way of producing a sane man? He is somewhat tired of trying political remedies for the cure of human ills. He knows that when the Roman Republic became corrupt, men sought to cure it by making it an empire; and when the Stuart kings of England grew tyrannical, men fled to America and founded a republic; but neither Rome nor America gained much more liberty than if all had remained untouched. So the guildsman turns to more fundamental factors than political constitutions. He turns to a time when man was mainly a craftsman and a democrat who had not wasted many hours on politicians and governors.

There is a moment when patience with our opponents is no longer a virtue. We have sat submissive too long while the salesmen of these modern ideals have dogmatically announced their wares. There is a moment when it is time to say quite curtly that we have listened enough to this insolent bluff—for half this defence of the modern state is bluff and nothing else. When we are offered for our homage a society which gives us Sir Edward Carson[48] instead of Becket,[49] and *Comic Cuts*[50] instead of illuminated manuscripts; a society which has built Liverpool and New York and destroyed Ypres and Reims; which has set up plutocracy in black coats instead of aristocrats, who at least knew how to dress; which has given us millionaires instead of the millennium, and factory hands and smoke for a peasantry who at least could see the sun; when, in short, we are offered unmitigated nonsense for something that at least had romance and beauty and an unaffected common sense; then it is time to show our opponents the door and suggest the nearest gatepost as a more suitable companion for their confidences. Tolerance is a very great gift, a very great virtue; but when men say they are talking sense when they are flying in the face of all the facts, then it is time to show a little human dignity.

Our opponents imagine that they have answered us with the crushing phrase, "We cannot go back to the Middle Ages." It would be equally pertinent to reply that the charge of the Light Brigade[51] would be a pastime for nursery maids compared with the superb heroism of riding much farther with the present system.

However, we do not desire to return. We merely wish to cling to the fundamental facts of human nature, rather than to flirt with some idle fancies that flitted through the heads of a few economists and politicians who mistook statutes and ballot boxes for the wisdom of mankind. We are not the sentimentalists; it is the man who says that Birmingham is a greater city than Bruges who is giddy with sentiment – and regardless of facts. But if he really means that he does not want to return to Bruges even if he could, then we can touch ground in the debate. We are not quarrelling about methods; we are struggling over the root principles of human existence. It is not a matter of social machinery; it is a question of morals, of taste, of elemental sanity. We do not pretend that the guild system will give the "modern" man what he is seeking. At least we pray most devoutly that it will not, for if it does, it will be but another of those unkind tricks by which a mysterious fate has so often made sport of mankind.

THE SEAL OF THE DUBLIN
GUILD OF ST. LUKE

NOTES

1. Wat Tyler (1325–1381). Leader of the Peasant Revolt that took place in Kent, England in the period 1381–1382. The 100,000 or so peasants who took to arms demanded that the excessive taxation that was applied to them be lifted, that serfdom be brought to an end, and that the oppressive labor laws be abolished. King Richard II, granting their demands, brought an effective end to the revolt and most peasants retired home, but Tyler, heady on the mixture of power and menace, pushed his demands ever further with the result that he was captured and executed, and the previous agreement annulled.

2. John Ball (?–1382). Coming under the influence of Wyclif, he went amongst the peasants as a priest arguing in their favour and demanding ecclesiastical poverty for the priesthood. Thrown into prison for his activities, he was released by English peasants in 1381 who were revolting under the leadership of Jack Straw. Once released he continued his activities, but he was eventually captured and hanged, drawn, and quartered.

3. Myrtle Villa. Probably a reference to the residence of Sir William De Stancy, a character in the 1896 novel *A Laodicean: A Story of Today* by Thomas Hardy (1840–1928). Taylor's expression is a criticism of the bland "respectability" and "mushroom modernism" (to use Hardy's words) of suburbs such as were even then in development, supplanting the old, natural, integrated, and organic life and architecture of the earlier towns and rural communities.

4. Mr. Paton. Probably a reference to John (?) Paton, an advocate of the national guilds as proposed by G. D. H. Cole. Paton had a regular column, "Notes of the Month," in the magazine, *The Guildsman*, and was secretary of the Glasgow group of the National Guilds League.

5. James Watt (1736–1819). Scottish mathematical instrument maker. Developed the famous Watt Steam Engine which was granted a parliamentary patent, thereby giving it a virtual monopoly. Became immensely rich. Richard Arkwright used Watt's engines in his textile sweat factories, and between 1781 and 1800 Watt sold more than 500 of the engines.

6. Poosie Nancy's. A tavern in the village of Mauchline, Ayrshire, Scotland. It was the watering hole of Robert Burns (1759–1796) and where he wrote "Love and Liberty." It is believed that he first sang "Auld Lang Syne" there, and that its rapid spread was due to Scottish Freemasonry, of which he was a member, according to the tenor of the article "Auld Lang Syne and Brother Robert Burns" in the *Scottish Rite Journal*.

7. Emily Caroline Gibson Townshend (1849–1934). An advocate of the guild system in the post-WWI period; member, until 1915, of the Fabian Society, and a founder that same year of the National Guilds Leage (of which she was also treasurer). In a March 1918 issue of A.R.Orage's influential journal, *The New Age*, she wrote of G.D.H.Cole's "consumer state" that "[it] repels me by reason of its materialism." Her dislike of such materialism naturally pushed her towards Penty's more "spiritual" view of the guilds and of life. Besides *The New Age*, she contributed to *The Christian Socialist*, *The Guildsman*, and *Everyman*. She translated from the Italian a useful book on fascism by Odon Por, with whom she maintained a not infrequent correspondence and who was a reference also for Penty on the guild system in Italy. Her other works include *Creative Socialism* (London: J. M. Dent & Sons, Ltd., 1924) and several Fabian Society pamphlets. It is perhaps not insignificant that she died at Ditchling, in Sussex, England. G.R.S.Taylor wrote of her in the obituary he penned for the London *Times*: "She was always the youngest mind in any circle . . . . Nothing could stop her energy, and there was no end to her desire to know the world and its human inhabitants."

8. Arthur Joseph Penty (1875–1937). English architect and Christian social thinker. He was a member of the Fabian Society from 1902 until 1916, but it was always a turbulent relationship, since he opposed their collectivism. It served, however, to develop his social thought. Under the influence of Ruskin, Arnold, Carlyle and Morris, he came to realize that the industrial arrangement of society was both brutal and futile. He came to believe that regulative guilds were the answer to contemporary problems, since they combined cooperation with individual initiative, private property with the common good, and efficiency with the moral and spiritual. Described by G.K.Chesterton as "the greatest of the Distributists," he wrote profusely. Works include *The Restoration of the Gild System* (1906), *Old Worlds for New* (1917), *A Guildsman's Interpretation of History* (1920), *Post-Industrialism* (1922) and *Distributism: A Manifesto* (1937).

9. William the Conqueror (1028–1087). Duke of Normandy whose kingdom was the most powerful vassal of the French Crown of the day. Following the victory over the Anglo-Saxons in 1066, he was consecrated King of England in Westminster Abbey in 1067, though revolts broke out in Exeter, the Welsh Borders, and Northumbria immediately afterwards. The revolts were suppressed violently. William greatly improved the condition of the Church in England.

10. King John (1166–1216). Brother of the famous crusading king, Richard the Lionheart. He usurped his brother's throne during his absence in the Holy Land, but fled when Richard returned. John became king in his own right in 1199, but his succession was disputed by Arthur of Brittany. The ensuing war meant that by 1205 he had lost most of his French lands, in spite of the massive amount of money that he put into the campaign and raised by heavy taxes in England. Such taxation led to his unpopularity with almost everyone, and his dispute with Pope Innocent III over the nomination of Stephen Langton as Archbishop of Canterbury merely rounded things off. He was excommunicated in 1209, but was rein-

stated when he repented in 1213. In June 1215, rebel barons seized London and John was forced to draw up his now famous Magna Carta—the basis of English law—which outlined the rights and duties of the Crown and its main subjects.

11. The Waldenses. Members of a heretical sect founded by Waldes, a wealthy merchant from Lyons, and which appeared in the twelfth century. They were also known as the Leonistæ and Sandaliati. It still exists today though in a highly modified form. It spread quite quickly from France to Italy and then Spain, but its adherents were largely ignorant folk. The preaching confraternity that began in 1176 eventually had to be suppressed in 1184 by Pope Lucius III because the preaching was contaminated by heresy, and persuasion had produced no fruit. The secular authorities took a harder line from 1192. By then they had come to deny purgatory, five of the seven sacraments, prayers for the dead, and indulgences. The Italian Waldenses were always rather insular, so that they survived when most of the other groups merged into the Reformation that erupted in the sixteenth century.

12. Winston Churchill (1874–1965). Son of Lord Randolph Churchill, he fought in the Sudan against Al Mahdi in 1898. While on active service he wrote *The Story of the Malakind Field Force* (1898) and *The River War* (1899). Began working for the *Morning Post* in 1899, but in 1900 became a Tory M.P. Became a Liberal in 1904 because he found himself more in agreement with Liberal views on social reform. He became First Lord of the Admiralty in 1911, and set up the Royal Naval Air Service in 1912. In dealing with a rebellious Iraqi population in 1918 he said: "I am strongly in favour of using poisoned gas against uncivilized tribes to spread a lively terror." He was Prime Minister 1940–45 and 1951–55. Written works include *Liberalism and the Social Problem* (1909) and *The History of the English Speaking Peoples*. He won the Nobel Prize for Literature in 1953.

13. St. Anselm (1033–1109). An Italian who became an Archbishop of Canterbury and was proclaimed a Doctor of the Church by Pope Clement XI in 1720. A man of great intellect and humility, he never sought preferment. He ended up in England when he became the Abbot of the Monastery of Le Bec in France in 1078, and thus had to visit its lands in England. His governance stood for the defence of the Church's freedom against the encroachments of the secular authorities. Works include *Monologium*, *Proslogium*, and *Cur Deus Homo*.

14. Lord George Curzon (1859–1925). A Tory M.P. from 1886, but he was more interested at that stage in travelling the world for material for his books than in Parliamentary work. He was the Secretary of State for India from 1891–1894, and Viceroy of India from 1898. During the period 1919-1924, he was the Foreign Secretary, whilst in the Lords he founded the Anti-Suffrage League in an attempt to block votes for women. Works include *Russia in Central Asia* (1889), *Persia and the Persian Question* (1892) and *Problems of the Far East* (1894).

15. There are a number of Simon de Montforts who have made history. It is probable that Taylor's reference is to the Simon de Montfort whose birth date remains unknown, but who died in Toulouse in 1218. He became Baron de Montfort in

1181, and took the cross in 1199 after hearing Fulk de Neuilly preaching the crusade in the province of Champagne. Unfortunately, the French knights went off at a tangent and the Pope's plans for the Holy Land were frustrated. De Montfort became the Earl of Leicester in 1204, but his main concerns rested with France. In 1208 he was appointed Captain General of the crusade to eliminate the Cathar heretics in the south of France. He demonstrated great military skill and swept to victory. Although he was intrepid and sincere in his Catholicism, he was greatly marked by bad faith, excessive cruelty in war, and treachery.

16. English Heptarchy. The term was first used by Henry of Huntingdon, and it refers to that period in English history following the Anglo-Saxon conquest but before the Viking invasion. Thus, it is the period between 500–850. In Greek the word *heptarchy* means "seven rulers," the rulers in this case being the kings of England's seven kingdoms: Northumbria, Mercia, East Anglia, Essex, Kent, Sussex, and Wessex.

17. Henry Tudor (1457–1509). The founder of the Tudor dynasty, he became Henry VII of England when he defeated King Richard III, of the House of York, at the Battle of Bosworth Field in 1485. This brought the War of the Roses between the Houses of York and Lancaster to an end, but his claim to the throne was highly questionable. In order to maintain his position, he divided the opposition through coercion and bribery as well as marrying off sons and daughters at home and abroad. This way he gained money, alliances, and time. He is "credited" with having introduced an efficient tax system.

18. Louis XI (1423–1483). French king who was a born diplomat. He managed by great skill to check both his foreign and domestic enemies through the setting up of an efficient bureaucracy, and by allying himself with the lesser nobles, the bourgeoisie, and the lower classes. He greatly expanded his kingdom, and enormously increased industry and domestic and foreign trade.

19. Elizabeth I (1533–1603). Elizabeth Tudor, Queen of England, daughter of that Henry VIII who broke with Rome over his demand for an annulment – and which led, as a result, to the foundation of the Church of England. No friend of Catholicism, nonetheless Belloc could say of her, in his *Elizabethan Commentary,* "We must remember her isolation, her lack of anything that could support her soul, her lack even of what people in her position have a right to demand, the security of the future."

20. William Cecil (1520–1598). The first Lord Burleigh was ennobled in 1571 by Elizabeth I, and in 1572 became Lord High Chancellor. He was appointed Chief Secretary of State by this queen in 1558, and for the next forty years he was the main architect of her religious and political policy: a policy at once anti-Catholic and pro-rich.

21. Francis Walsingham (c.1530–1590). Son of a prosperous merchant, he became a fervent supporter of Protestantism whilst studying at Cambridge. He entered the House of Commons when Elizabeth I came to the throne, thanks to the patronage of William Cecil. In 1573, he was made the Principal Secretary,

specializing in foreign affairs. In this role he sought to intervene militarily in Europe on the side of the Protestants, but he was reined in by Cecil. He created during his life an intricate network of agents and informers so as to possess what we would now call "intelligence."

22. David Lloyd George (1863–1945). Elected Liberal MP in 1890, President of the British Board of Trade in 1906, and Chancellor of the Exchequer in 1908. Implicated in the Marconi Scandal of 1912–1913; broke with progressive Liberals in 1914 as a result of his refusal to oppose Britain's entry into World War I. Appointed Minister of Munitions in 1915; was Prime Minister from 1916 to 1922.

23. Plantagenets. A line of English kings from the Houses of York and Lancaster, which spanned 331 years beginning in the twelfth century. The name "Plantagenet" was not used until the mid-fifteenth century, though its origin lay with the father of Henry II (king from 1154 to 1189), Geoffrey, Count of Anjou. The Count used to wear a sprig of flowers upon himself as a badge, hence "planta genista."

24. 10 Downing Street. The official residence of the British Prime Minister in London.

25. Reform Act of 1918. A reference to the 1918 Women's Act, brought in by the Asquith government, which granted the franchise to women who were over the age of 30, householders or wives of householders, occupiers of property with an annual rent of £5, or British university graduates. Although a number of women stood as candidates in the 1918 General Election, only one, Countess Markiewicz, representing Sinn Féin in Ireland, was elected.

26. The Entente Powers. The military alliance, though never at any time formal and driven only by a variety of interrelated treaties, comprised of France, Russia, and Britain. It started with an accord between Russia and France in 1894, and was later joined by a Britain concerned about the growing strength of the German Navy. The Entente was opposed by the Central Powers – mainly Austro-Hungary and Germany although other nations were also "allied" – with the result that pre-WWI Europe was, practically speaking, dominated by two highly armed military blocs.

27. A *mir*. Russian word to describe the pre-Soviet village community or commune.

28. *Gens*. A word with Greek and Roman roots which signifies a group of families with supposed common origin, sharing a name and religious rites. One might use the word "clan" as an approximation.

29. Sir Henry James Maine (1822–88). English jurist and historian educated at Cambridge. He believed that the history of laws was the surest guide to the study of the history of civilization. His influence on the history of jurisprudence is incalculable, and he warned that democracy and progress were not necessarily the same thing. His works include *Ancient Law* (1861), *Village Communities in East and West* (1871) and *Popular Government* (1885).

Notes

30. *Cyrano de Bergerac*. A play by Edmond Rostand (1868–1918), first produced on December 28, 1897, in Paris. De Bergerac is a guardsman and poet who is cursed by a huge, bulbous nose. He believes that no woman would ever come to love him because of it, so he made himself renowned for personal courage and charm.

31. *Morning Post*. Daily newspaper founded in 1772. Initially employed notable writers such as Samuel Coleridge, Robert Southey, William Wordsworth, and Charles Lamb to improve its status and circulation. Purchased by Sir James Berry, owner of the *Daily Telegraph*, a paper founded in 1855, and still being published; contrary to Berry's original intentions, the two papers were quickly amalgamated.

32. Heinrich Heine (1797–1856). German Jewish poet who wrote *Lorelei*, which was set to music by Silcher in 1837. He was taught by G. W. F. Hegel in Berlin, and was a great admirer of Napoleon; this admiration influenced his work.

33. Hottentot. A member of a southern African Negroid people which formerly occupied the region near the Cape. The name comes from the Afrikaans language for "stammered," and refers to the Hottentots' peculiar mode of pronunciation.

34. Joseph Conrad (1857–1924). Born Jósef Konrad Korzeniowski, he became Joseph Konrad when he was naturalized a British citizen. A Polish noble, he became a novelist, short-story writer, and adventurer who travelled widely as a seaman. It was on his long sea voyages to Latin America and South East Asia that he began to write, though this ceased when he inherited the equivalent of £100,000 in 1894. Works include *The Nigger of Narcissus* (1897), *Lord Jim* (1900), *Heart of Darkness* (1902), and *Nostromo* (1904).

35. El Dorado. A reference to a fictitious city or country abounding in gold, or a place of great abundance. It derives from the Spanish *el dorado* meaning "the guilded."

36. Hugh Capet (c. 944–996). Founder of the Capetian line of French kings, he was before that a powerful duke with lands near Paris and Orleans. Closely allied to the German emperors, he was elected by the nobles and thanks to the intervention of the Archbishop of Rheims upon the death of the Carolingian king Lothair.

37. Whitley Reports. In the immediate aftermath of WWI, John Henry Whitley (1866–1935), a Liberal member of the British Parliament, following the acceptance of his recommendations to the House of Lords concerning contemporary economic problems, instituted the Whitley Council. The Council was formed with the intention of setting up a consultative committee or organization in a company or industry, and which drew representation from both management and staff. The purpose of the Council was to discuss pay rates, working conditions, industrial relations, and work-related issues. A multiplicity of such Councils now exists in England, though they are of a purely reformist nature.

38. *cul-de-sac*. French for "dead end."

39. Fabian. A member of the Fabian Society. This organization was founded in 1884 to bring about a Socialist state, not through armed insurrection or violence, but by incremental politics, piecemeal legislation, and peer-group pressure.

40. Honoré Balzac (1799–1850). French novelist and writer who helped create the trend of realism in literature. He wrote a large number of novels and short stories, many of which were collected together in *The Human Comedy* in 1842. Other works include *La Cousine Bette* (1846) and *Les Chouans* (1829).

41. *Tu n'as donc pas de mère*. French for, "So you don't have a mother!"

42. Alexander the Macedonian (356 B.C.–323 B.C.). Better known in history as Alexander the Great. He became King of Macedonia in 336, and launched his campaign in 334 to punish the Persians for their previous invasion of Greece. His campaign took him to Persia, Syria, Egypt, Afghanistan, and India. Major victories were had at Chaeronea (338), Tyre (332) and Megalopolis (331). He died preparing an invasion of Arabia.

43. Jay Gould (1836–1892). An American speculator who rose from humble origins to be a railway magnate and owner of the Western Union Telegraph Company. The attempt by Gould and James Fisk to corner the gold market in 1869 caused the "Black Friday" panic. The *Columbia Encyclopedia* says, "For years his name was a symbol of autocratic business practice, and he was widely disliked."

44. Andrew Carnegie (1835–1919). Scottish-born industrialist who set up the Carnegie Steel Company in Pittsburgh in 1865, which he sold in 1900 to J. P. Morgan for $400 million. In 1889 he wrote *The Gospel of Wealth*, in which he asserted that all personal wealth that went beyond one's reasonable needs should be used for the benefit of the community. He set up, as a consequence, a series of foundations to promote philanthropic and educational projects. By the time of his death he had given away some $350 million.

45. George Meredith (1828–1909). Issue of a poor family, he rose to be regarded as one of the finest poets and writers of the Victorian age. His first volume of poetry was published in 1851.

46. Robert Grosseteste (c.1175–1253). Teacher, philosopher, and man of letters who rose to become Chancellor of the then relatively new university at Oxford. He was reputed to have been one of the most learned men of the Middle Ages, with great interest and knowledge in Theology, Mathematics, Hebrew, Science and Music. A good friend of the Franciscan Order, he became the Bishop of Lincoln, England's largest diocese, in 1235.

47. Tokay. A sweet, aromatic dessert wine made near Tokaj in Hungary.

48. Edward Carson, Lord of Duncairn (1854–1935). Protestant lawyer who became MP for Trinity College, Dublin, in 1892. Violently hostile to Irish Home Rule, he became leader of the Irish Unionist Parliamentary Party in 1910. Supported the paramilitary gun-running efforts of the Ulster Volunteer Force, and was in favour of the Partition of Ireland.

49. St. Thomas à Becket (1118–1170). Following a life of great ups and down, he became Lord Chancellor to Henry II of England in 1154. He was very close to the King and whilst a mere deacon personally went into battle. A Cistercian, he was ordained on June 2, 1162, and consecrated a bishop the day after. Thereafter he was in constant tension with the King, who sought, as Thomas saw it, the aggrandizement of the kingdom at the expense of the real interests of the Church. When confronted by four knights who had come to kill him–whether at Henry's bidding or not is not clear–they asked, "Where is the traitor?" to which he replied, "Here I am, no traitor, but archbishop and priest of God." Killed in his own church, devotion to him spread so quickly that by 1173 he was canonized by the Pope. In 1174, Henry II did public penance, being scourged at St. Thomas's tomb.

50. *Comic Cuts* (1890–1953). A children's newspaper, created by press baron Alfred Harmsworth (1865–1922), later Lord Northcliffe. Its success was partly due to the fact that it sold at half the price of its predecessors.

51. *The Charge of the Light Brigade.* A poem written by Alfred Lord Tennyson (1809–1892) to commemorate the suicidal English light cavalry charge at the Battle of Balaclava (1854) in the Ukraine during the Crimean War (1854–56) when Britain, Turkey, and France were pitted against Russia. Of the Brigade's 637 men, 247 were killed or wounded. Its opening lines are famous:

> Half a league, half a league,
> Half a league forward,
> All in the valley of Death,
> Rode the Six Hundred.

Titles New & Old from IHS Press
are available direct from the publisher or at fine bookstores.
Order yours today. ─────────────────────

The Outline of Sanity, by G.K. Chesterton
184pp, 6"x9", ISBN 0-9714894-0-8, Item No. GKC001 **$14.95**

The Free Press, by Hilaire Belloc
96pp, 5½"x8½", ISBN 0-9714894-1-6, Item No. HB001 **$8.95**

Action: A Manual for the Reconstruction of Christendom, by Jean Ousset
272pp, 6"x9", ISBN 0-9714894-2-4, Item No. JO001 **$16.95**

An Essay on the Restoration of Property, by Hilaire Belloc
104pp, 5½"x8½", ISBN 0-9714894-4-0, Item No. HB002 **$8.95**

Utopia of Usurers, by G.K. Chesterton
136pp, 5½"x8½", ISBN 0-9714894-3-2, Item No. GKC002 **$11.95**

Irish Impressions, by G.K. Chesterton
152pp, 5½"x8½", ISBN 0-9714894-5-9, Item No. GKC003 **$12.95**

The Church and the Land, by Fr. Vincent McNabb
192pp, 6"x9", ISBN 0-9714894-6-7, Item No. VM001 **$14.95**

Capitalism, Protestantism and Catholicism, by Amintore Fanfani
192pp, 6"x9", ISBN 0-9714894-7-5, Item No. AF001 **$14.95**

Twelve Types, by G.K. Chesterton
96pp, 5½"x8½", ISBN 0-9714894-8-3, Item No. GKC004 **$8.95**

The Gauntlet: A Challenge to the Myth of Progress, A first anthology of the writings of Arthur J. Penty
96pp, 5½"x8½", ISBN 0-9714894-9-1, Item No. AP001 **$8.95**

Flee to the Fields, the papers of the Catholic Land Movement
160pp, 5½"x8½", ISBN 0-9718286-0-1, Item No. FF001 **$12.95**

An Essay on the Economic Effects of the Reformation, by George O'Brien
160pp, 5½"x8½", ISBN 0-9718286-2-8, Item No. GO001 **$12.95**

Charles I, by Hilaire Belloc
288pp, 6"x9", ISBN 0-9718286-3-6, Item No. HB003 **$16.95**

Charles II: the Last Rally, by Hilaire Belloc
224pp, 6"x9", ISBN 0-9718286-4-4, Item No. HB004 **$15.95**

A Miscellany of Men, by G.K. Chesterton
184pp, 5½"x8½", ISBN 0-9718286-1-X, Item No. GKC005 **$13.95**

Distributist Perspectives, Vol. I, by the chief Distibutists
96pp, 5½"x8½", ISBN 0-9718286-7-9, Item No. DP001 **$8.95**

Dollfuss: An Austrian Patriot, by Fr. Johannes Messner
160pp, 5½"x8½", ISBN 0-9718286-6-0, Item No. JM001 **$12.95**

Economics for Helen, by Hilaire Belloc
160pp, 5½"x8½", ISBN 1-932528-03-2, Item No. HB006 **$12.95**

Richelieu, by Hilaire Belloc
272pp, 6"x9", ISBN 0-9718286-8-7, Item No. HB005 **$16.95**

Neo-CONNED!, by Pat Buchanan, Jude Wanniski, Sam Francis, et al
447pp, 6"x9", ISBN 1-932528-04-0, Item No. NC01 **$25.95** (hardback w/ dust jacket)

Neo-CONNED! Again, by Robert Fisk, Robert Hickson, Donn de Grand Pré, et al
897pp, 6"x9", ISBN 1-932528-05-9, Item No. NC02 **$29.95** (hardback w/ dust jacket)

Order direct today: by phone, fax, mail, e-mail, online.
s/h: $3.50 per book; $1.50 ea. add'l. book. Check, m.o., VISA, MC.

toll-free telephone or fax: 877-IHS-PRES (877.447.7737)
e-mail: order@ihspress.com • *internet:* www.ihspress.com